10 SPIRITUAL PRINCIPLES *of* SUCCESSFUL WOMEN

Victoria Lowe

HARVEST HOUSE PUBLISHERS

EUGENE, OREGON

Cover by Koechel Peterson & Associates, Inc., Minneapolis, Minnesota

10 SPIRITUAL PRINCIPLES OF SUCCESSFUL WOMEN
Copyright © 2004 by Well Said LLC
Published by Harvest House Publishers
Eugene, Oregon 97402
www.harvesthousepublishers.com

Library of Congress Cataloging-in-Publication Data

Lowe, Victoria, 1961-
10 spiritual principles of successful women / Victoria Lowe.
  p. cm.
ISBN 0-7369-1393-9 (pbk.)
1. Christian women—Religious life. 2. Success—Religious aspects—Christianity.
I. Title: Ten spiritual principles of successful women. II. Title.
BV4527.L68 2004
248.8'43—dc22   2004005751

Printed in the United States of America

04   05   06   07   08   09   10   11   / DP-MS /   10   9   8   7   6   5   4   3   2   1

This book is dedicated to my mother, Climmie Lee Davidson, who raised me to be a woman of integrity. Her love and prayers have carried me safely from one side of this country to the other.

Mom, thanks for passing on your sweet spirit.
You are a very special woman.

I love you with all my heart!

Victoria

$\mathcal{A}$cknowledgments

With Special Thanks:

To my Lord and Savior, thank You for entrusting me with Your precious words. I will forever be grateful for the privilege of sharing *10 Spiritual Principles of Successful Women*. You have a servant for life.

To Briana and Nikki, my loving daughters, thank you for allowing Mommy to fulfill my destiny. Briana, thank you for sharing me with the world. I will always appreciate the time you lovingly gave Mommy to write this book. I am so proud of you and Nikki. You are beautiful young women God will use in mighty ways.

To Mom, Dad, and my sisters, Vanessa and Venita, thank you for loving me so unconditionally. Mom, thank you for teaching me that love really is the way. Your love, support, and confidence have given me the strength to press past difficult times. Now God can trust me and use me. Thank you!

To Pastor Paula White and your dynamic team at Paula White Ministries, thank you for your collaboration. Paula, my spiritual soul sister, thank you. You are fabulous. God is using you and your team in a mighty way. It is an honor to be your friend. I look forward to working together as we allow God to use us to save souls and build the kingdom.

To my Harvest House family: Bob Hawkins Sr., Bob Hawkins Jr., Jennifer Ekwere, Carolyn McCready, Terry Glaspey, Kimberly Shumate, John Constance, Julie McKinney, Katie Lane, Teresa Evenson, the editorial team, and the entire staff, thank you. I will forever be grateful for your belief in me. Your dedication and colossal talents brought my dream to life. I know millions of people will be blessed by your sincere efforts. Thank you for producing books that give God all the honor and glory. Terry and Carolyn, you put the "team" in team spirit. Thank you so much.

To Hope Lyda, thank you for taking my words and developing them into clear pictures for the readers. You were a delight to work with. Thanks for keeping me inspired all the way to the very end. Your hard work and the editorial department's detailed labor brought the words to life.

To my Alert Staffing family, thank you for your patience and love. I could not have completed this book without your support. Thank you for allowing me to stay focused. I will always remember the small things. Roy Gardner, my right hand, you are an angel sent from heaven!

To my pastor, Bishop Kenneth C. Ulmer, and Lady T, thank you for your friendship. Pastor, thank you for teaching the uncompromisable Word of God so clearly and concisely to me for over 14 years. Your work has not been in vain.

To Ron Finley, thank you for your support throughout this project. You're always there, pressing me to keep going. As you would say, "can't stop, won't stop."

To my prayer partners Clotee, Alice, and Mother Alice (the Host of Heaven), thank you for always being there to pray, encourage, feed, and pick me up from the airport. You will always be family to me. Alice, thanks for picking Briana up from school so I could stay focused on finishing the book. I know God will bless your Al Mac Wil music project because of your tremendous talent and servant's heart. Angie, thank you for the financial blessings. God used you!

To my friend Shirley Blair, thank you for your prayers and unbelievable friendship.

To *all* my friends who have prayed and given me encouragement along this new and exciting journey, thank you from the bottom of my heart. You have sown seeds into my life that will produce a tremendous harvest. I will never be the same. Thank you for believing in me!

Contents

Foreword

God engineered you to be a success, but do you really know what success means? And do you know how to get there? Many women today spend their lives searching and hoping to accomplish, acquire, and achieve what the world defines as success. For some of us, our life quest has become the hunt for financial independence or career accomplishments or a stable family. Yet, even when we achieve the things the world describes as success, we are often left feeling unfulfilled. This is because we cannot be fulfilled without accomplishing what God has already ordained as our life mission. I am convinced that true success is birthing every dream God has placed inside of you so that you can live at your fullest potential.

In this powerful book, Victoria Lowe reveals biblically sound principles that will unleash the greatness God has planted inside of you. She offers a scriptural roadmap to chart the journey to realizing your destiny, while equipping you with God's Word to encourage and strengthen you along the way.

It has been scientifically proven that a bumblebee cannot fly. Its wingspan is far too short to carry its weight. The problem is, nobody ever told that to the bumblebee. This book will position you to see the many ways God has already prepared you to fly, regardless of what the world has told you.

What are you going to do with the life you have left? By the time you finish this book, you will not only know, you will have a plan to start today! Victoria Lowe is a gift to the body of Christ and to women around the world who have miracles inside just waiting for practical steps to give birth to them.

You have been raised up for such a time as NOW. Don't miss your moment!

Paula White

$\mathcal{M}$y Story

"Your testimonies are wonderful; therefore my
soul keeps them."

PSALM 119:129

My journey began in St. Louis, Missouri. I was born to parents with big hearts and entrepreneurial spirits who taught me that you only get out of life what you invest in it. I have two beautiful sisters, and I grew up shielded between them as the middle child. From this position in the family, I was able to be an observer, taking my time to absorb knowledge about life and relationships.

My spiritual journey was a long and difficult trip. As a young child I was involved in going door-to-door distributing the *Watchtower* and *Awake*—materials of the Jehovah Witness church. It took me many years to untangle my spiritual confusion. From the time I came out of college until I landed in Chicago, I was on an all-out search to find the one true God. But after a while I was tired of searching; I wanted to give up. It was easier to just stay out in the world and have fun. Still, something inside of me would not let me quit. There was a burning fire to have God in my life.

Although I was baptized in Chicago, my daily walk with God did not begin until I was in Los Angeles and attending Faithful Central Baptist Church, now known as Faithful Central Bible Church, pastored by a great teacher of the gospel, Bishop Kenneth C. Ulmer. Because of his dynamic and uncompromising teaching, I was able to build a rock-solid foundation on the Word of God. My life was also changed when I picked up Bishop T.D. Jakes book *Woman, Thou Art Loosed!* God used this book to free me of the physical and mental bondage I had been locked in since childhood. The message allowed me to pick up the broken pieces of my identity and turn my life toward God's purpose. The season of forgiveness I experienced led me to a more meaningful, spiritual life. Truth is…I felt alive for the first time in years.

My first eight years on the West Coast were spent working for a national staffing company managing their Los Angeles region. During that time my husband and I chose to start a family, and within months I was pregnant with my first child. Still young in my Christian faith, I had not yet faced the tests that refine one's beliefs. But that was about to change. Early labor contractions placed me in the hospital and at the Lord's mercy. A turning point in my faith took place in that hospital room—I heard God whisper. God spoke and said, "Victoria, I wanted to get your attention. You have turned every aspect of your life over to Me except your career. I have allowed you to be successful in every way. Now I have work for you to do. I tried to get your attention, but you were just too busy, so I sat you down for a minute." Like many naïve Christians, I bargained with God and said, "I will go where You say to go and do whatever You tell me to do. I promise to be obedient and available to You." And in that hospital room God reassured me about the health of my baby and His plan for my life.

I had heard people say God spoke to them, but I thought they might be fabricating the details a bit. So I was amazed that God was speaking so clearly to my spirit. I sensed a shift was taking place in my life and my faith. From then on I would pray with the knowledge that God was very present and very involved in my life. And in my heart. I could not wait until He spoke to me again.

Just a few months after my beautiful baby girl was born, God spoke again and told me I was supposed to start my own staffing company because He had plans to bless it and take it far quickly. He said the overall purpose would not be about business success but about fulfilling my purpose for ministry. To my heart He spoke, "I am doing a new thing. I will give you unusual success quickly. You will have access and relationships with people and corporations instantly that take most business owners decades to build. But do not get confused. I am positioning you for the work of the kingdom." This was all very overwhelming. Was I really up to starting a business right then? As I looked at my precious little girl, Briana, I remembered my promise to God in the hospital…to be available to Him and to be ready when He said it was time. He was saying "now is the time."

I was worried that I did not have the faith to do what God told me to do. I kept calling Yolanda, a friend and prayer partner, to talk everything through. The week of decision came; I either had to go back to work or tell them I would not be back. I told them I would not be returning. They were very unhappy with my decision, and I was quite anxious about it myself. When I hung up the phone, I began to panic. *What have I done?* I started pacing the floor. I walked up and down the hallway praying, "Lord, please tell me I just did the right thing."

The following week my friend and business associate Carin Maher and I launched the company with 20 thousand dollars we borrowed from family members, friends, and credit cards. We used my living room the first four weeks to get ourselves organized while we searched for office space. Early one morning I stood in my living room with my robe on and a cup of coffee in my hand looking out the large, front window. I reflected on all we had accomplished over the last couple of weeks and pondered what our next couple of weeks would consist of. It was then that I heard God's voice. He softly whispered in my left ear, "Eyes have not seen nor have ears heard what I have for you." It was as if He were leaning on my left shoulder with His hands around my ear. My heart started to beat fast, and I began to cry.

I was overwhelmed with the outpouring of love my heavenly Father was showing me. I felt as though I had just buckled myself into one of the big roller coasters at an amusement park. I knew the ride would move at high speeds, and we would scream and holler along the way. There would be twists, turns, and dips, and most of the time we would not be able to see what was coming next, but at no time would we be in any danger. I was excited about all of the possibilities that lay before me.

The business took off right away. The first year our revenues exceeded a million dollars. I had been reading a lot about joint ventures and partnerships. Many articles said a joint venture or partnership is the best way to grow your company, so we put a marketing piece together and went out and partnered with the largest staffing company in the world. Within the first year I knew the deal was in trouble. We were not sharing any deals and the services we were receiving from them were not working out at all. By the second and third year we were still partners, but each company had cut off communication and gone their separate ways. While we were out growing our business quickly for our size, my partners were out purchasing company after company. Their annual revenue reached more than 13 billion dollars within three or four years. Our company, in an eight-year period, expanded to revenues of more than 100 million.

Even with all that growth, my international staffing partners decided I was not running the company the way they felt I should, so they wanted to replace me. They attempted to discredit my company and myself. I was devastated. I thought partners worked together. They accused me of everything, from stealing money to taking kickback from the money I had paid to my church. I got a real lesson in just how cold big business could be. I think they underestimated the little business and person they were taking on. I had a great team behind me, and my parents had taught me to stand up for what is right and fight if you are forced to. Well, I had the fight of my life on my hands. The battle lasted over three years, costing the company a small fortune in legal fees, and in the end the court found that we had done nothing wrong.

I saw the hand of God not only pull us out of bankruptcy but also sustain our reputation and our customers, and He allowed us to start three new companies. We came out alive but not without wounds. Our revenues had gone down to less than ten million dollars. And yet through it all God gave us favor with incredible attorneys like Angela Sousa and John Gibson, who saw the corruption in the bankruptcy system and stood by us through thick and thin. We also had faithful clients who stood beside us through the entire three-year battle. I will always be grateful to them for their trust and support. The battle was not over because now we had to rebuild. But I knew I served a God who was bigger than a bankruptcy and bigger than corporate America.

Even before the legal matters were resolved, I had to face the sorrow of the dissolution of my marriage. It was at this time that God whispered softly in my right ear, "for such a time as now." When I heard the whisper it sounded familiar to me. It took me back to the time when God had whispered in my left ear back in my living room. Now He was whispering in my right ear. So I put them together: "Eyes have not seen nor have ears heard what I have for you, for such a time as now." I looked up to heaven and wondered, *What does all of this mean? What is God trying to tell me?* In the face of such personal and professional loss, I knew I had nowhere to go except to follow God's leading.

Eager to figure out what God had for me, I followed His lead to Pastor Paula White's conference in Florida. It was there that He told me it was time to start my ministry. I did not question His input. I had seen God moving so much on my behalf while building my company and bringing me through the court battle, I knew I was not to question His plan. When I returned to Los Angeles, I began developing the spiritual principles and planning the seminar He had placed on my heart.

After going through so many battles, I prayed often for a ministry that focused on teaching Christians how to live successful lifestyles; a ministry designed to help us operate and grow our businesses. I longed for answers to what I perceived to be difficult questions. How can we live successful lifestyles God's way? I did not realize I had the answer right in front of me. The power of prayer and applying God's Word through spiritual principles was the answer to my question.

The spiritual support and education I longed for during all my trials was nowhere to be found. All along I had no idea God was preparing me to build the very ministry I was looking for. He allowed me to go through trials and tribulations to equip me to serve Christian women. Because of His directive hand, I am now armed to support the woman who is looking to stay at home and raise her children, the woman who is determined to climb the corporate ladder, and the woman who is looking to raise up a business or ministry.

In a matter of months I was walking across the stage at my seminar to launch my new ministry based on the testimony and spiritual principles God had given me. What an awesome God we serve! As I said earlier, the rebuilding process has not been easy. There have been hundreds of hiccups along the way, but I stand trusting God to be my Jehovah-jira (the Lord will provide).

My journey has been challenging and rewarding all at the same time, but I thank God for every challenge and battle that has come my way, because it is through my adversity that He has developed my character. It is through my challenges that He has prepared me for my destiny. When I think of how this little Missouri girl has become an anointed woman of God who is being sent out into the world to spread the gospel, I can't help but shout out, "Glory to God!" I can't help but worship Him for who He is and praise Him for what He has done for me.

Deep in my heart I have a sense of all that God is doing and plans to do in your life—a life of purpose, vision, and blessing. For that I give Him the glory as well. We are sisters…we are fellow travelers…along the journey toward real success.

$\mathcal{W}$hat Is Real Success?

Success. Can you picture it? Is it far off in the distance and out of focus? Or is it vivid and in living color? Reflecting on a clear picture of real success allows us to discern our purpose, clarify our vision, and recognize the blessing of success along our journey. A successful woman holds this picture in her mind, heart, and spirit. The effect is a bit like posting a photo of our "slim days" on the refrigerator door: A picture of success gives us determination when we are weak, encouragement when we stumble, and kudos when we are faithful.

What Success Is Not

Let us take a moment to look at what success is *not*. Though I am an optimistic person, I start with the negative because, sadly, that is the most common image conjured up when women are asked, "How do you picture success?" Our minds—educated in the classroom of the world—often envision luxury cars, lots of cash, breathtaking views from private verandas, and fancy houses (and these joys, of course, coincide with the return of our "slim days.") These symbols of "making it" are by-products of a certain kind of success, but they are not success. Success is not material bounty. Success is not measured by the rungs of the corporate ladder. Status, promotions, and company expense accounts are not requirements for living an abundant life. However, as a person thrives in her God-given purpose and vision, financial growth can follow. For this reason I will address the responsibilities tied to material blessings as we journey through ten spiritual principles. A well-grounded faith and a heart of purpose turn possessions and monetary riches into opportunities for stewardship and real success.

The Simplicity of Success

My definition is simple, powerful, and everlasting: Success is attaining total peace and fulfillment in every aspect of your life. At certain seasons in our lives, this might sound as unrealistic as "success is winning the lottery twice." But there is a very encouraging difference. A lottery win is dependent upon the unreliability of luck and our random numeric guesses. Real success depends on the reliability of our awesome God and our deliberate spiritual principles.

The Journey to Success

I have discovered five keys to real success: 1) have peace with yourself and your life, 2) commit to excellence, 3) operate with a servant's heart, 4) pay the cost, and 5) know what season you are in.

Have Peace with Yourself and Your Life

We must have peace with ourselves about our lives at all times. True peace as described in Philippians 4:7 is that which "surpasses all understanding." Worldly peace is contingent upon the known happening...everything going as planned. Smooth sailing. This version of peace gleams with perfection in our mind's eye, and there it stays, a glossy image that never takes dimension in our daily existence.

But what about when things don't go according to the plan? When real-life circumstances take their everyday twists and turns? Only true peace can rise up and comfort us. Only true peace can give us the total reassurance that everything really will be all right. Once we learn to rest in this peace, wholeness and fulfillment begin to take shape in our lives.

Peace with yourself and your circumstances (ideal or not) begins with God. When He becomes your Lord, the journey to total peace begins. Then the peace that "surpasses understanding" can reside in your life when everything is wonderful and when everything seems to be falling apart.

Commit to Excellence

Real success only comes to a person who is committed to excellence. Success, in bottom-line terms, means to complete something we set out to accomplish. And excellence ensures that our pursued picture of success is in line with our God-given best. If we allow a "this is good enough" philosophy to enter our system of values, we end up with a very diluted version of success. And, sadly, such success will not look anything like the plan God has for you. It will be incomplete instead of whole. It will be disappointing instead of fulfilling.

We must keep our eyes on the prize and align our steps with the end goal. Determination to finish fueled by faith protects us from discouragement and intimidation.

Operate with a Servant's Heart

Greatness is measured by service, not status. A successful woman serves God's purpose rather than her own vanity, ego, or personal agenda. We can all nod in agreement at that statement. We realize God is more important than we are. But this next part trips us up every time: Success is found while bowing at the feet of others. This shocking image goes against everything the world teaches us about success and fulfillment. And yet it is familiar. This revolutionary, extraordinary image matches an impression in our spirits. It is the image of Jesus. This, my friend, is the picture to hold in your heart.

"Whoever wants to become great among you must be your servant" (Mark 10:43 NIV). If you want real success that is everlasting, you must become a full-time servant of the Lord. I do not mean quit your job and go into full-time ministry (unless this is your vision). God calls us to a personal ministry that flows through our company jobs, our parenting style, our homes, and into the lives of others and into the world.

Pay the Cost

The cost of reaching your goals can be very high; therefore, our journey toward success molds our testimony of faith. The greater the testimony, the greater the test. Following the principles of success is like building a house. You put up the frame, you add the drywall, you stack the bricks one by one. Many people don't want to build a house because it takes a lot of time, money, and work. Success requires the same level of investment. God requires us to pay our own way of small sacrifices so we will not be quick to jeopardize the journey by taking shortcuts or using false materials.

The price of success can include time, effort, and even some friendships. Cost involves an exchange of one item of value for another. Determine what you are willing to invest of your heart and soul in order to receive the success God has for you. The One who paid the ultimate cost showed us that a successful journey requires a toll of adversity and perseverance before you are able to move forward in your purpose.

As we pay the cost required, we must look at our offerings as God does. In her book *Walking on Water*, Madeleine L'Engle writes, "Often we forget that he has a special gift for each one of us, because we tend to weigh and measure such gifts with the coin of the world's marketplace. The widow's mite was worth more than all the rich men's gold because it represented the focus of her life. Her poverty was rich because all she had belonged to the living Lord."[1] If your bank account holds three dollars, you have as much ability to give as a rich man. It is about sacrifice. Paying the cost is about giving to the Lord the focus of our lives.

Know Which Season You Are In

Oftentimes we want to leap to the season of harvest, forgetting that God first calls us to seasons of preparation and sowing. If you do not accomplish what needs to happen in a particular season, you will remain in a time of waiting. While you wait for God, God is waiting for you to learn about yourself, about Him, and about the blessing of the season that is upon you. Accomplishing the necessary tasks will allow you to move on to the next season. You can plant an orange tree in a cold climate, but it will not grow. If you invest in a version of success that is not meant to take root in your life's garden, you will not see fruit. Know who you are, what season you are in, and pray for wisdom to know which seeds to plant.

I strongly believe you have the opportunity to be successful in every season of your life if you follow in God's will. Align your expectations with His purpose and be willing to do the appropriate work for the season you are in. And just as the fruit comes forth in the appropriate season, your blessings will spring forth when their time has come.

Real Success Is...

Real success is discovered only after hard work.

Real success asks you to know who you are and who you are not...what you are willing to do and not willing to do. Your road to success begins with a step toward God's will. From there, you can walk in His purpose and your vision.

Real success is getting to a place where circumstances do not dictate your identity or your sense of peace.

Real success requires faith that you are where you are supposed to be. It does not matter how much money you have in the bank or where you live. Whether you live in a mansion, your mother's house, or subsidized housing, if you are pursuing God's best for your life, your today is leading to your tomorrow.

Real success is following His strategic plan for your life. Everything you experience prepares you for a fruitful future. Successful people understand that where they are today is not where they will be staying. You are on your way to someplace great. At a conference I attended, Bishop T.D. Jakes said, "Water your own dreams—no one can water your dreams but you. You must shed your own tears of struggle. Once the struggle ends, your garden will be beautiful." Today is the best day of your life, and tomorrow is going to be even better. Real success already belongs to you because you have the victory in Jesus Christ!

Real success is falling in love with God, sharing that love with others, and opening your heart to the manifestation of love's return.

PART ONE:
Purpose

SPIRITUAL PRINCIPLE

*T*rust God's Will

*Line up with God's desire for your life
and rest within God's perfect will.*

"Do not be conformed to this world, but be
transformed by the renewing of your mind, that
you may prove what is that good and acceptable and perfect will of God."

ROMANS 12:2

It was a Friday afternoon, and the sun illuminated a room filled
with brightly colored construction paper, miniature chairs, activity
stations, and signs welcoming myself and others to career day at
my daughter's school. As part of the activities, each child said what
they wanted to be when they grew up. I couldn't wait to hear how
these young children pictured their futures.

One by one they stood and presented their dreams of a future
self. Out of 20 children, there were eight wannabe doctors, three
attorneys, four movie stars, and five other occupations mentioned.
Their reasoning went a bit like this: "I want to be a doctor-
celebrity-lawyer because they are important and make a lot of
money." At least 15 of the children described success as making
a lot of money.

These kids had already bought into that "not" version of success. Silly me, I figured we all took on those ungodly views of success as we entered college or the workforce or just adulthood in general, but that day I realized most of us have carried around a worldly lie in place of a spiritual truth since kindergarten. How can God's will take hold of our hearts when we are giving them away at age six?

I kept looking over at my daughter's face while all the other children were speaking. She seemed a little confused. When it was her turn, she said she might want to be a teacher but really did not know for certain. I was proud of her courage to say she did not know. My desire for Briana and Nikki has always been for them to receive a great education and be able to take care of themselves, but first and foremost I want each of them to be living out her purpose and walking in God's will. In the classroom that day, my daughter's "I don't know" meant her heart was still open to God's plan.

Over the years I have spoken to many doctors and lawyers who were in the middle of changing careers. And when I ask why, the answer is invariably the same: "My job as a doctor-celebrity-lawyer is not fulfilling. I am not happy." These men and women have carried around that naïve success myth in their back pocket all these years. They brought it out and read it like a map, never asking God if the picture resembled the picture He had for them.

And what do these people want to do now? Open a flower shop, become a parent, work with humanitarian agencies, start a home business so they can be around their families…the list goes on. I realize people change as they mature. It does take time to get to know ourselves and our purpose, but if we would just focus on God's will from the start, I think we could avoid many of the wrong paths. I would bet many of these people in transition are headed toward the life God intended for them all along.

Are you following the map God has placed on your heart, or are you still trying to figure it out for your self?

Where Are You?

Where are you right now? Are you in God's will? Are you happy? Do you get up every morning feeling as though you are headed down the right road? Or have you taken so many different turns you are not sure anymore? I hate to break it to you, but if you have passed the same milestone four times in the past five years, you might just be wandering in circles.

There is no better time than this moment to make a quick analysis of where you are in life and determine if you need to make some changes. Are you ready to do the work involved in such an exploration?

I can remember when I felt as if my entire life were coming apart at the seams. I knew I needed to make some changes, but I did not have the energy to make them. I was going to church every Sunday, and it helped a little bit. But by Tuesday I was right back in my rut again. I kept promising myself that next week I would begin exercising, reading my morning devotions, setting goals. Have you ever noticed how "next week" never comes?

I maintained the household and put in my time at work, but the thrill was long gone. I was functioning on autopilot.

Then one week I decided to go to the Wednesday evening service at my church. Running a bit late, I arrived just as the speaker was standing to speak. His first words were, "Are you living in God's perfect will?" I really did not know how to respond. But his question led me to ask myself, "Victoria, are you happy?" My answer was obvious.

The speaker spent the next 40 minutes sharing information and Scriptures with us. I wrote down as much as I could in my journal. And that night when I got down on my knees to pray just as I did every night, something stirred in my spirit. I was different. Just spending one hour contemplating God's will had moved me from a place of fatigue and discontent to a place of desire for a righteous, godly life.

I asked God to help me. I asked Him to show me how to live in His perfect will. *Show me how to live this life the speaker talked about tonight. Show me how to live in total prosperity.* I spent the next several weeks researching God's Word regarding His will and found a wealth of information that changed my life! May it serve to move you forward in your journey.

God's Perfect Will or Your Free Will

The first thing I discovered is that God is a God of choices. He gives us a free will to choose our paths and live with the destination and the outcome. We receive the opportunity to choose whether we will walk with Him on the side of goodness or whether we take the chance of walking on our own, where Satan is out there waiting to steal, kill, and destroy all the blessings God has for you.

I had been trying to find my own way long enough by the time I attended that Wednesday night service. I was covered with spiritual bruises from fighting the attacks of the devil. And my mind played a tune of resolution over and over. *No more. No more. Show me the way, Lord.*

His Perfect Will for Our Lives

God's desires for our lives were clear from the beginning. He equipped us from the beginning to be successful. After He created heaven and earth, He made man in His own image so we would be distinct from all the other creatures. He gave us authority over the earth and everything on it. And He provided characteristics we need to become successful, including intelligence, creativity, and inspiration. Because of the value God has invested in each of us, we should strive to be the best we can be and reach the highest level we can reach. To do less is to be unfaithful to the life God has entrusted to us. We should never accept anything less than what God has made possible for us to achieve.

His Heart's Desire

"I have come that they may have life, and that they may have it more abundantly" (John 10:10). It is God's will that we live in abundance. Abundance means overflowing, more than enough, extraordinary, more than sufficient. I become excited when I think about the life God intends for each of us to have.

His desire is for us to prosper. Third John 2 says, "Beloved, I pray that you may prosper in all things and be in health, just as your soul prospers." The prosperity God calls us to is born out of commitment, dedication, and action that is in line with His word. The Greek word for "prosper" used in this Scripture *(euodoo)* literally means to succeed in reaching. It implies that prosperity is an ongoing, progressing state of success. The prosperity journey happens step-by-step in the spiritual, physical, emotional, and material aspects of our paths.

Psalm 1:3 says, "He shall be like a tree planted by the rivers of water, that brings forth its fruit in its due season, whose leaf also shall not wither; and whatever he does shall prosper." Not only is it God's will for us to prosper as individuals, but it is His desire that everything we do will prosper. It is His desire for our family, children, marriage, business, ministry, job, and health to thrive. God's perfect will is to bless us because He loves us so much. There is no good thing that He wants to withhold from us.

Obedient to His Word

Our obedience to God's Word allows us to walk in His ways toward the success He has planned for us. That sounds like a great deal…and it is, but this path to success involves commitment on our end as well. Our end of the bargain is to uphold His Word on a daily basis. God shares His will through His word. We are to embrace His Word and know it intimately. Once we begin to study and explore the Bible, we will find reference and instructions to almost every situation and circumstance in our lives.

The Purpose of His Will

My journey had to start with a very difficult first stop…the altar of God. It had to be done if I was truly ready for God's success. God was giving me a clear picture of what His altar was created for. I used to think the altar of the Lord was a place of renewal and covenant. A place of life. But first, God's altar is a place of death. Death must take place before the miracle of resurrection can follow. To be obedient to this requirement, I needed to bring my will to the altar so it could be destroyed.

To lay myself on the altar, I spent my time fasting and praying. God showed me everything that had to die: my self, my pride, and the toughest of all…my dreams and desires that were not aligned with His will.

My dream and desire was to grow a billion-dollar international staffing company that would provide employment for people all over the world. I saw myself traveling around the globe as a corporate executive meeting with other executives of large organizations and corporations. While this is a nice dream, and the beginnings of it had been within God's will, the end destination was not.

At the time of my company's bankruptcy battle, I could not clearly see that the battle was not about salvaging a business, keeping clients, and saving our jobs. The battle was the manifestation of God's plan for our lives. God used the bankruptcy to move me and others on my team toward our destinies. The difficult circumstance provided me with experience I would need to fulfill my destiny. God knew that I would not take the time to evaluate where I was in relation to His will until I learned the lesson of obedience and submission. The company I grew from my living room, the company that was near and dear to my heart, had to be pushed off track to move me from my corporate life to my ministry life. God knew I needed a nudge. A big nudge.

God's plan to send me around the world was not for corporate achievement, but to empower and educate His people. But to give in to His desire for my life meant I had to put my will and desire on that altar daily. I felt as if I were being pushed to do something I did not understand and did not have the experience to do. You have been there too, haven't you? God is very interesting. He tends to put you in situations that you are not equipped to handle so you can see His mighty hand at work. We cannot take the credit because God's presence and will are so evident in our circumstances. Our lips and hearts must praise Him.

The Battle Is His

I pray that in the midst of your struggles you will see that "the battle is the LORD's" (1 Samuel 17:47). The battle really is not even about us. I don't mean to say we do not have responsibilities in our circumstances...after all, we still must hold to integrity. But the spiritual impact of your situation is beyond just your life, your needs, your failings, your victories; the battle is about kingdom business. The devil would like to stop you from completing your destiny because he knows your success glorifies the Lord. You see, God uses us as instruments to complete kingdom business. We need to stop worrying so much about situations and start focusing on what God is trying to do. We need to find the answer to the question, "What is God trying to make happen through us? Through this trial?"

When you go to the altar with your life, your struggle, and your personal will, you surrender to the One who knows the path you are to take. He is the Alpha and the Omega. He knows the beginning and the end...and the journey in between.

Walking in His Will

Children do not learn to walk without being shown how. So must we be shown how to walk in God's will. Let's look at Romans 12:1-2:

> I beseech you therefore, brethren, by the mercies of God, that you present your bodies a living sacrifice, holy, acceptable to God, which is your reasonable service. And do not be conformed to this world, but be transformed by the renewing of your mind, that you

may prove what is that good and acceptable and perfect will of God.

While we are standing at the altar, we are called to keep giving until our entire selves are presented to the Lord. Our physical body, focus, attitude, behavior, and thoughts become a living, holy sacrifice. That is no small task. Many of us have trouble submitting to authority of any kind…from landlords to traffic cops to supervisors. But when we submit and surrender our whole selves to the Lord, we do so in the strength of His mercy. It is not by our power alone.

These verses in Romans call us to be transformed by the renewing of our minds. Do not copy the behavior or customs of this world, but be transformed into a person of new thoughts, of godly thinking. We become transformed into this new creation by changing the way we think. The negative thinking of old dies in order for our minds to be reborn. I call negative thinking "stinking thinking." When you study and reflect on God's Word and His promises, this stinking thinking will fall away. Again, it requires obedience and sacrifice, but we cannot be rebuilt from the inside out until the old, useless parts are identified, removed, and replaced.

When I was in college I pledged a sorority. During the pledging process one of my big sisters would often ask me to do an attitude check. This process required me to do a quick analysis of my thinking and attitude and report my findings back to her. My answer was always good, because if I did have an attitude problem it was fixed by the time I answered. We need to identify our stinking thinking and correct it because our attitude and what we think determines who we are and how receptive we are to God's will.

We must not allow the circumstances of life to dictate our thoughts. We must begin thinking like our Father in heaven, who always thinks good things for us. The troubles and fears of this world do not confine Him. He gives us the same freedom to think far beyond the limitations of this world by imagining the impossible to be possible.

Paul encourages us to be transformed by the renewing of our minds so that we "may prove what is that good and acceptable and perfect will of God." To prove means to prove in practice daily that God's will for us is good and acceptable and perfect. We practice every day by choosing to be committed to the ideals of the kingdom. Once we decide to live this way, God makes us a promise. He promises that if we give all of ourselves to Him, then everything He has for us is good and perfect and everlasting. An anonymous writer once wrote, "The will of God will never take you where the grace of God cannot keep you."

Through experience and time I have come to the realization that everything valuable and lasting must start with God's will for our lives. The only way to achieve real success is to be aligned with what He has for us. His desires assure us that we will find real happiness and fulfillment in life that will be eternal. Exchange the world's temporal offerings of status and money for the eternal blessings God has stored up for His children.

Principle Prayer

Lord, I come to Your altar with my humble offerings. I bring to You my will, my life, my body, and my every thought. I am under Your authority. Give me eyes to see those areas that I hold on to out of stubbornness and ignorance. Release me from the grip and temptation of temporal life so that I can embrace eternal blessings. I praise You for receiving my sacrifice. I praise You for taking a life of little and transforming it into a life of abundance. Amen.

𝒫rinciple in Practice

1. If your map to success is left over from kindergarten (or was created before you became a Christian), throw it away and seek His Word to find your way forward.

2. Are you happy? Are you living in God's will? Ask yourself the hard questions because they lead to a thirst for godly living.

3. List or think of a dozen characteristics God gave you to be successful. Thank Him.

4. Is the fruit of your life prosperous? If not, examine why your work, home, family, and relationships are not thriving.

5. Have you been to the altar lately? Prepare your whole self and life to be a living sacrifice.

6. Sacrifice negative thinking and "prove what is that good and acceptable and perfect will of God" (Romans 12:2).

*E*mbrace Water-Walking Faith

*Be willing to get out of the boat of safety
and move toward your destiny.*

"For we walk by faith and not by sight."
2 CORINTHIANS 5:7

When I think of the kind of faith God wants us to have, I think
of the story in Matthew 14:22-33 and Peter's request to walk on
water. I envision Peter and the other disciples out to sea on a
crowded boat. Jesus was on shore because He had gone to the
mountainside to pray. Meanwhile, a storm brews and blows across
the sea. When Jesus descends the mountain, He sees the boat
rocking in the wind. Nothing extraordinary. Not yet.

I see the disciples huddling together, their faces filled with fear
and frustration because they don't know what to do. As they look
out into the rush of rain against the night sky, the form of Jesus
emerges. It is the Savior walking toward them on the surface of
the water. Rather than feel relief, the disciples are more fearful
because surely this must be a ghost. No man can walk on water.

They forgot that this man was the Son of God. With courage that comes from faith and a touch of adrenaline, Peter makes an interesting request once he realizes this is not an apparition. He asks Jesus to call to him. He wants to walk on water. Can you imagine asking to get out of the boat…at night…during a storm…to walk on water? How many of us would be cowering and fretting rather than asking for a personal miracle?

Ask for a Miracle

Not only did Peter want to *see* a miracle, he wanted to be the leading character *in* a miracle. I love this! He is witnessing the miraculous as he sees Jesus coming toward him, but he understands that he too can experience this miracle in a personal way. That is faith, my friend. That is water-walking faith.

Peter, unfortunately, also models what many of us would do in such a situation. He goes from strong belief to a moment of fear just as Jesus is giving him the miracle. "But when he saw that the wind was boisterous, he was afraid; and beginning to sink he cried out, saying, 'Lord, save me!' And immediately Jesus stretched out His hand and caught him, and said to him, 'O you of little faith, why did you doubt?'" (Matthew 14:30-32). We cannot really fault Peter. After all, when we feel the pressure of the world—the winds of criticism or doubt—we often take a look at our miracle and think, "This miracle must be all in my mind. Save me, Lord!"

We can learn a lot from Peter. His first desire was to trust in the Lord. And his first response was to ask for that miracle. How often do we make a general request to God to save us from a circumstance, trial, or the unknown, rather than asking for a specific, personal miracle? The problem is, we don't fully believe. Not really. We praise God. We see blessings in our lives and are thankful.

We ask for the winds of change and turmoil to be calmed so we can paddle to shore and get back to safety. Yet we forget to ask for the extraordinary. We neglect to trust God completely with our lives. Our miracle stops with the shift in weather just when the real adventure of the faith life is beginning.

Don't you want to be the one who steps out of the boat with faith, conviction, and amazement? Is a storm brewing in your life today? Are you facing black sky and torrential rains right now? Face your situation as a water walker. Ask for what you need, gather the hem of your garment, step over the bow and onto the waves, and believe. Water walkers claim victory every day.

Is the Water Safe?

Safety is not all it's cracked up to be. Whether it is your personal or business life, remaining on the boat might feel like the wise decision. After all, your peers are there, your coworkers, and anyone else who says, "This is the way everyone else is doing it. It must be right." But this safe, conscious decision to stay in the boat allows the movement of the wind and water to direct our lives rather than the movement of the Holy Spirit. The safe choice might lead to our destination—the shore—but our journey is limited by fear, worry, and weak faith, a lifeless journey compared to the one that overflows with the passion of belief. To live as a water walker is to experience real success.

Experience Complete Trust

Our struggle with trusting God may be a direct result of our inability to trust others in our lives. This is perhaps a "which came first, the chicken or the egg" point of debate. But either way you vote, a lack of trust in one area is likely to affect the other.

Many of us have been let down or disappointed by others enough times that we have learned to guard our hearts. So we ignore the response to trust anyone. Soon our relationships, our jobs, and even our churches seem to be filled with people who have made and broken promise after promise.

I was sitting in my family room one day looking out of the window at blue sky and clouds. I do not recall what situation I was in the middle of, but I remember thinking, *Whom do I have in my life that I can trust? How many people do I have in my life that I can count on?* As I sat there gazing out the window, I tried to come up with names. Outside of some family members, the list was short...and each name came with stipulations or conditions because my faith in each person carried the baggage of doubt, past experience, and overall lack of trust. Perhaps the most striking realization was that the name with the longest list of conditions and disclaimers was *my own*. It was clear that I placed little faith in myself—the person I should trust the most along my life's journey.

I Am Not Worthy

I believe many women have "I am not worthy" conversations with themselves. We don't need someone else telling us what to do or how we fall short of expectations; we manage this on our own. While we should be supporting ourselves with encouragement and belief, we turn into self-abusers. We feed our hearts verbal, emotional, and spiritual lies that counter our value in God.

The conversation goes something like this: *I go to church every Sunday or I used to, but I can't seem to find the answers to my questions. I listen to the message, take notes, and even buy the tapes and listen to them over and over again. I pray, but I am not sure God is hearing my prayers. I am always praying about what I need and want while there are people who are homeless, going to bed hungry, and dying in the streets. Why would God waste His time listening to my prayers? I feel empty and lost. I have not told anyone because I am embarrassed. I'm one of the people who are supposed to have it all together. I am really tired. All these big dreams about having success, family, great responsibility, respect…I must be crazy. Nothing seems to be happening. Every time I look up it is New Year's again, and all the plans I made for this year remain on my to-do list. I just keep living day to day, surviving not thriving. I want more out of life, but I am not sure how to get it. I know God created me for His purpose, but I am not sure I have what it takes to accomplish what He wants me to do. I have made so many mistakes in life. I keep falling down, getting up, and falling down again. My body, mind, and spirit are weary. My failures cause me to doubt everything I know about myself and about God. I don't deserve what He has for me. Because of my mistakes and sin, I don't feel worthy of His blessings. Where do I find success in the middle of my failures? Where do I put my faith? Whom can I trust completely?*

After a recent conversation like this one, I spent time in deep prayer. I prayed fervently, desperately, and with a pleading heart. I wanted to better understand how to have faith. I revisited the words of a father who pleaded for Jesus to rebuke the demon that possessed his son. "Jesus said to him, 'If you can believe, all things are possible to him who believes.' Immediately the father of the child cried out and said with tears, 'Lord, I believe; help my unbelief!'" (Mark 9:23-25). This is such an amazing response from the father. It is as revealing as Peter's request to walk on water because, even as this man believes and asks for a personal miracle, he acknowledges his unbelief. You see, even in the midst of deep faith, most of us murmur this request for God to help our state of unbelief. And Jesus does not turn us away.

Making Room for Belief

Our hearts become imprisoned by our past mistakes, failures, and self-doubt. There is no room left for value, belief, and faith. During one of those "I am not worthy" conversations, I felt God's love leading me to confront everything I was holding on to as truth instead of His truth. I thought back on bad decisions, errors, and moments of pride and jotted them down on paper as a way to purge them from my spirit. I felt deep regret over some things I had done and over certain things I had not done. In that moment of sadness, I heard a still, small voice inside of me saying, "Let it go, Victoria." With great relief I tore up that piece of paper with my handwritten list of past mistakes. As my body emptied itself of long overdue tears, my heart was released from its captivity of lingering past sins.

The new Victoria arose from the ashes of her past. When I thought about spiritual principles, such as integrity, vision, and gratitude, I no longer heard the protesting cries of doubt; I heard God say, "I have healed you in your unbelief. And you are free."

Our complete faith and trust should only be put in God. Not in ourselves or anyone else. He wants to handle every aspect of our lives, our personal and business affairs. God is powerful enough to hear every prayer and deal with all circumstances. As our Father, He is concerned about everything that affects us. He gave us the Bible and the church because He knew we would feel lost at times and alone. We are all broken vessels in need of God's loving hands to continue to mold and shape us into the perfect vessels He desires.

One day while Jesus was in the temple courts, some teachers and Pharisees brought before Him a woman who had been caught in adultery. They challenged Jesus with a question. "Now Moses, in the law, commanded us that such should be stoned. But what do You say?" (John 8:5-6). Jesus rose up and said to them, "He who is without sin among you, let him throw a stone at her first" (John 8:7). The Bible tells us that the people there, young and old, were convicted by their own conscience and left one by one. Then Jesus faced the woman and spoke words many of us have studied in Scripture numerous times. "He said to her, 'Woman, where are those accusers of yours? Has no one condemned you?' She said, 'No one, Lord.' And Jesus said to her, 'Neither do I condemn you; go and sin no more'" (John 8:10-12).

While God continues to mold and shape us, we will fall from time to time. The issue isn't whether we will fall but rather what we do after we have fallen. Romans 3:23-24 tells us that we have all sinned and fall short of God's standards, yet God in His gracious mercy declares us not guilty. He has forgiven us of all our sins and shortcomings. Now it is time for us to forgive ourselves. Time to press forward and renew our mind, body, and spirit. "Trust in the LORD with all your heart, and lean not on your own understanding" (Proverbs 3:5). Leave your understanding and your weary spirit in the old season and by faith walk into a new season with strength and power and trust.

God has a purpose for our lives that will fulfill our dreams. "The very hairs of your head are all numbered" (Matthew 10:30). If the hairs on our heads are numbered and considered worthy of mention, then certainly our dreams and desires are important to Him. We are His children, and because of Him we are worthy. We are worthy to accomplish and receive everything He has for us. Everything He has for you will come to pass. It does not matter what anyone else says or does. Within our own strength we may not be able to handle the ups and downs of a day, week, or month... but God can. He wants us walking by His side through every circumstance and situation we face. We are to invite Him to come in to reign and take charge of our entire life. He will be a true friend no matter what we are going through. We can come to Him anytime or anyplace. There are no special directions and rules we must abide by in order to approach God. We come as we are. And He is faithful.

Learning to Walk by Faith

When you live in constant communication with God and with walk-on-water faith, your senses and your actions become more significant because you are moving forward in His purpose and toward your personal vision. We will explore both purpose and vision in more depth, but I wanted to take a look at how your physical senses and actions reflect what is going on spiritually.

Faith by Listening and Hearing

Our spirits must learn to listen to what God is saying. This is a skill that is learned by spending time with God and investing in a relationship with Him. We know we have a close friendship with a girlfriend when we can finish a sentence she starts, can answer her question before she can put it in words, or know exactly what she is thinking by reading the look on her face. When we reach this level of communication, we intuit nonverbal messages and can recognize the person's voice without seeing them.

This is the type of relationship we must build with God. When He moves through the Holy Spirit, we are aware of it; when He speaks quietly from within or through others, we recognize His voice. Following directions is an important part of living by spiritual principles. When our spirit can discern God's voice, we can walk in faith forward in our purpose because we know it is from Him.

Eight years ago when I stood in my living room with my baby in my arms, God whispered in my left ear to inform me that the company I was to build would be a national staffing company. I could have questioned that, but I had a relationship with God. I knew His voice. I moved forward by faith, trusting Him to do what He said He would do. And He was true to His word.

Faith does not have to feel like a guessing game. As you walk obediently in His will, His voice will assure you again and again of His love and authority. When your spirit is listening, your steps will be certain.

Faith by Speaking

The tongue is a powerful tool that we can use for good or evil. We can speak light and deliverance into someone's life, or we can communicate darkness and death. Our words can be used to love and support or hurt and destroy. In our effort to become open communicators, many of us say whatever comes to mind, all for the sake of honesty. However, we must measure our words carefully. An unkind word is not like an ill-fitting sweater…you don't just take it back. We can clarify and apologize, but our spoken words are out there forever. Psalm 34:13 tell us to "keep your tongue from evil, and your lips from speaking deceit." Our tongue can be used for wicked purposes, and it has the power to ruin people's lives.

We are to control the tongue at all times. It has been said that few sins exist that do not somehow involve the tongue. Whether we are the speaker of evil or the receiver of sin-filled words, there are many ways the tongue becomes a weapon of destruction. Gossip can destroy a foundation of trust overnight. Negative words born out of a negative outlook can steer us and others along paths of discontent and unbelief. Angry words become tools of intimidation and fear. "For God has not given us a spirit of fear, but of power and of love and of a sound mind" (2 Timothy 1:7). If we are living our lives espousing fear or living in fear generated by another's actions, our thoughts become crippled by doubt and indecision. God longs for us to have more. He created us with a spirit of love and security so we can be of sound mind.

God allows us to use our voice to speak blessings into being. Under His authority we can use our tongues to heal the sick and cast out demons. We can walk into dead situations and speak of life and forgiveness. I have wasted so much effort being politically correct when I was supposed to be spiritually correct. I used to express my heart in a very limited, world-approved way. I lived and acted by faith, but I was not speaking the language of faith until I began to openly share God's truth…even when it was not politically correct.

When we begin to speak life into our marriages, parenting, careers, and businesses, we understand the control God has given us through faith. We can take a stand and speak change into our lives. When we walk into a situation, we can declare by faith that we have victory over the situation. Whether we are praying for physical healing, interviewing for a promotion, or negotiating on a multimillion dollar contract, by faith we can speak victory.

God is waiting on us to release our faith so we can move mountains. Through faith God has given us authority and power. Matthew 17:20 says, "If you have faith as a mustard seed, you will say to this mountain, 'Move from here to there,' and it will move; and nothing will be impossible for you."

Faith by Application

God is looking for people who will choose to walk by faith. People who will get up in the morning trusting and believing God to make a way out of no way. Trusting Him to use the same power He used to raise Jesus from the dead in our situations. To bring dead deals back to life, to keep our lives moving forward even when the doctor has given us a bad report or there is no money in our bank account. How much faith do you have? Many of us read about faith in our Bibles and hear about faith in our churches. Many times God has already told us what to do to turn a situation around, but the answer seems unbelievable. We do not have enough faith to believe what God has already told us, but faith the size of a mustard seed is all it takes to bring our lives from surviving to thriving.

In many cases we apply faith in our personal life but not our professional lives. I think this is because we are trained to believe we get where we are by our own ability. Women especially take pride in achieving career goals without handouts or favoritism. But don't be fooled for one moment…God got you to where you are today. And He will get you to where you are supposed to be tomorrow. If we face a crisis…now that's when we get on our knees and acknowledge who is in charge. That is when we ask God to send help right away. "Lord, will You come quickly? I need You."

Real faith allows you to step onto the water and receive miracles. Are you trusting God in all areas of your life and during the good, bad, and ugly times? Once we walk by faith and not by sight, previously closed doors open…or new doors appear along a path that felt restricted and fruitless. The phone will begin to ring with new opportunities. The impossible will become the possible.

Pray over every decision…from marriage to buying a house to choosing a job. Keeping your faith mobile through an active prayer life helps you feel God's direct involvement at every turn. Before you go into a business meeting or a presentation, stop by the rest room so you can take a moment to ask God to go before you in the meeting. Ask Him by faith to give you favor with the individuals you will be meeting with and then step back and watch His mighty hand rule and reign over the meeting and decisions. When you walk in the room, they will be looking at you differently. If you are bold enough to ask, God is bold enough to grant your request.

Nothing is too simple or hard for God. With living faith, nothing is too hard for you to believe. Invite God into your decision-making process. Trust me—you will need Him when the battles come, and the battles will come. It is a lot easier to be walking with Him by faith all along instead of trying to usher Him in once the battle starts. When the battle begins, God is already on the scene and the battle at hand is in the process of being won. I have learned to stand on the following Scriptures to prepare my heart for all circumstances:

> "God shall supply all your needs according to His riches in glory by Christ Jesus" (Philippians 4:19).

> "He Himself has said, 'I will never leave you or forsake you.' So we may boldly say: 'The LORD is my helper; I will not fear. What can man do to me?'" (Hebrews 13:5-6).

> "Yet in all things we are more than conquerors through Him who loved us" (Romans 8:37).

It is important that we participate in the process of life. What is the use of saying we have faith if we do not reflect that faith through our actions? When Abraham offered his son Isaac on the altar in Genesis 22, God saw that Abraham was living out his faith in fear of God, even when it required great sacrifice. When God dried up the Red Sea, the Israelites marched through it as though it were a desert. They accepted and participated in that miracle.

Don't you want the kind of faith that allows you to walk between walls carved out of the sea or to walk on the water? This is the time to jump out by faith and experience life outside of the boat of unbelief, trusting God by faith to let us live miracles in our everyday lives, trusting God to catch us when we fall. He promised that He would.

Principle Prayer

Lord, I see You on the water. You are forming a miracle in my life, and I ask You to call me by name to receive it. I will leave behind the boat with its cargo of past mistakes and struggles. Though the storm of life might rise and fall about me, I will keep my eyes on You, my Savior, and I will walk. If doubt ever causes me to sink, I pray for the strength to continue forth...and I will pray "help me in my unbelief." Amen.

*P*rinciple in Practice

1. Look at a current storm in your life. When you see Jesus against the backdrop of the turmoil, are you afraid? Or do you ask Him for a miracle?

2. Think of a time in your life when you have had water-walking faith. How did God honor that faith? When have you seen others live out their belief this way?

3. What ties you to the boat of unbelief? Make room for your miracle by looking at what holds you back and releasing failures, sorrows, losses, and doubts to the Lord.

4. Pray to be made worthy. And don't ever doubt your value again.

5. Consider five ways to speak and act out faith in your life. Observe how this impacts you, your circumstances, and those around you.

6. Embrace a spirit of love and security. Take two small steps away from your personal "boat" this week and see what life looks like as a faithful water walker.

$\mathcal{P}$ray Without Ceasing

*Spend time in God's presence to listen
and be led to an abundant life.*

"Let your gentleness be known to all men. The
Lord is at hand. Be anxious for nothing, but in
everything by prayer and supplication, with
thanksgiving, let your request be made known
to God."

PHILIPPIANS 4:5-6

Several years ago I started waking up at 5:00 in the morning.
Not because I set my bedside alarm for this unnatural hour, but
because my internal clock sounded. For days I responded as any
hardworking, tired woman would...I rolled over, covered my head
with a pillow, and searched for a position that would lead me back
to deep slumber.

No luck. I began searching instead for a remedy to this problem.

I exchanged my late evening meal for a "normal" dinnertime,
in case that bad habit was the culprit. I placed a notepad by my
bed, reasoning that if I could immediately write down the mental
monologues that awakened me in the wee hours, maybe I would
fall back to sleep.

Nothing eased my restless spirit.

I became frustrated because I could no longer control my sleeping patterns. And to add insult to injury, it seemed I had no one to blame for my wakefulness. My daughter wasn't a crying, hungry infant anymore. I wasn't receiving calls from distraught or insomniac friends. The neighbor's dog was not barking.

The view out my window frames a koi pond, a lush yard, and the soothing, postcard-worthy silhouette of the coastline off in the distance. But even these serene images became tiresome when viewed in the early hours. So much so that I finally followed the urge to get up and grab my Bible. Muttering "I cannot believe I am doing this," I put on my robe and slippers and headed downstairs.

A Wake-up Call to Prayer

I sat at my kitchen table, set my Bible in front of me, and spoke to God. *Show me the problem, Lord. Fix this problem.* As I continued to pray…and plead…I looked out the kitchen window just as darkness bid my part of the world adieu and light made its majestic, quiet entrance. I had witnessed the birth of a new day.

My tense shoulders eased into a relaxed position. I stretched my arms out wide and took a large breath of this "new day" air like someone just stepping outside of their tent after a night of camping. My body no longer resisted being fully awake.

My spirit lifted; gratitude filled my entire being. *Praise You, God.* I could feel the presence of the Holy Spirit. My heart and soul sensed His embrace. I heard God's voice whisper to me, "I wanted you to rise up as a new day was about to break and spend time with Me." It took how many restless mornings for me to get it? This was not about a *problem* or about my late night bowl of pasta! This life-changing morning encounter was about Him and

His love for me. The Creator of new days, new beginnings, and life plans loved me enough to wake me, nudge my spirit, call me to His side, and share a sacred moment of worship and conversation. We are so lucky to have such a God as this!

Join Me in the Prayer Closet

Well, as you can imagine, my grumblings, for the most part, have stopped. It is still sacrificial time, but now when 5:00 A.M. rolls around, I grab my Bible and head to my kitchen table because I know the reason for this longing in my heart. I call this my "prayer closet time." It is my time to meet one-on-one with the Creator. Quiet surrounds me; the morning sun does not yet shine through my purple kitchen curtains. There is no noise or chaos…just silence. How long has it been since you felt such peace? Once you grow accustomed to this solace, this sacrificial time becomes a luxury. You will wonder how you ever survived without it. Truth is, some of us are barely making it through our days, our lives. Prayer leads to God's will. Don't spend another day without a prayer closet of your own.

Here is the flow of my prayer closet time. I pull a chair up to the end of my country-style table, and with closed eyes I breathe in through my nose and out through my mouth. This breathing pattern allows me to let go of all those worries that tie me to the world's weight. My purpose is to step into the presence of God.

Listen First

The first part of my prayer is a request. Not my list of needs, but the opposite. I ask God to remove everything that is on my heart and mind. Next, I invite Him into my home. By home I mean my house as well as myself, my circumstances, my all and all. I invite His presence to fill my mind, body, and spirit. As I quietly praise and thank God for who He is and all that He has done for me, the Holy Spirit begins ministering to me. I have learned not to be in a hurry, because sometimes I must practice the art of waiting on Him. Just as He has to wait on me sometimes.

Often we question why we do not hear more from God. The answer is simple. We rarely spend time listening. Our mouths and hearts open up wide as soon as we think "time to pray," and everything spills out at once. Sometimes our needs, requests, and petitions for forgiveness rush out so quickly that they overlap in our minds. This mass unloading fills our time to download from God. Imagine Jesus sitting across from you in your prayer closet, and all you do is ramble, "A friend is dating a non-Christian. What should I do? My mother is sick and needs healing. I am up for a promotion that I want, but it would involve a scary move. What should I do? I want to find a way to serve my neighbors more; direct me to a specific vision for that. Oh goodness, look at the time! Help Yourself to whatever is in the fridge. I'm late for work."

I hate to break it to you, but that is *not* communication. We might feel good that day because we purged our sins and needs, but we did not enter into a time of communion with God. Our spirit did not sit still long enough to hear any of His responses or to receive anything He wanted to give us for that day. We missed the purpose of prayer completely. If you spoke like that to your girlfriends, I would give it a month before they stopped calling you altogether. And prayer is with your Almighty Lord. Examine the way you have been spending time with your Savior.

When I listen first, I find that most of those questions or concerns I had to share have already been addressed by God. He speaks to our needs and gives guidance in that time of listening and receiving. He offers exactly what you need to move within His will for your life.

When you first spend time in your prayer closet, you might feel the silence is too much to bear. Minister and author Renita Weems explains why God allows and makes room for the silence. "As with most great communicators, God knows that the point of silence and the pause between sentences is not to give the audience the chance to fill the silence with empty babbling but to help create more depth to the conversation."[1] Rest in knowing that you are not called to fill the silence, but to accept it as a gift of intimacy.

Sacrificial Time Leads to Success

Experience has taught me that prayer is one of the most important principles for achieving real success. The discipline of going to the prayer closet has revealed an important truth: Prayer is the key to moving our lives in a successful direction. If you are at all like me, the idea of investing in your prayer life seems potentially boring and repetitive. I thought I would always have to push myself to make the effort. To my surprise I found the time to be refreshing, fulfilling, and inspiring. And my quality time with God allows me to also spend quality time with myself. This is an important aspect to ponder, my praying friend: If you are neglecting personal time with your God, you are also neglecting time for yourself and your spirit. The more you know about your Creator, the more you will discover about the life He planned for you. All the self-exploration theories and books in the world cannot offer the insight revealed during daily communion with God.

After prayers of thanksgiving, I share everything about my life: from the mundane to the extraordinary, from the failures to the victories. At my kitchen table God holds me and works out my problems. His comfort envelops me like a mother's arms. Whether I am tired, confused, or broken, God uses this time to make things better. He assures me that my footsteps are ordered and every step I take is in His plan. This prayer time with God brings Philippians 4:5-6 to life: "Let your gentleness be known to all men. The Lord is at hand. Be anxious for nothing, but in everything by prayer and supplication, with thanksgiving, let your requests be made known to God." My prayer time helps me understand that no matter what I'm going through, everything will be okay. God is working things out in my favor.

It is this sacrificial time spent with my Father that carries me through my days and toward success. I no longer miss my favorite hours of sleep; they have now become my one or two favorite hours to be awake.

To my amazement I found myself more focused and organized. I began to see God's hand move in and through every aspect of my life. Prayer changed the way I worked, planned, and viewed life. Prayer truly has changed Victoria the person. I have literally been transformed into a new creature. I have always been a rather joyful person, but now I embrace life more fully. I savor and enjoy the journey...even the hard times because I know it is in the Plan. God's hand does not leave me.

The way I live and think has shifted to line up with God's Word and His purpose. All the pieces of the puzzle were beginning to come together and form a picture crafted by the Master Creator. Because of my journey to a deeper prayer life, I understand the transforming power of prayer. I want to share this with you. I hope this discussion leads you to a richer prayer life...and in turn, you will embrace a richer life. If you have empty places or spiritual poverty, they will be filled by the abundance of grace and the blessings of spiritual wealth.

Are you ready to be filled?

Pray Without Ceasing

Praying is one of the most important action steps we can take as Christians. "Rejoice always, pray without ceasing, in everything give thanks; for this is the will of God in Christ Jesus for you" (1 Thessalonians 5:16-18). Daily prayer is His will for us. Yet we can become so lost in the life we are trying to live that we forget the miracle and privilege of having direct access to the Creator of the world. "Evening and morning and at noon I will pray, and cry aloud, and He shall hear my voice" (Psalm 55:17). Now that I understand the purpose of prayer, I find myself praying throughout the day.

In the first church right after Pentecost, the disciples decided they had become so busy with other business that the church business was not being handled to their satisfaction. They chose seven deacons to care for the church. The disciples' primary job description? To focus on prayer and ministry of the Word. Prayer was listed as their first priority because the disciples understood they must protect the church from the attacks of the devil. Was your initial thought, *How nice to have prayer your assigned job! Now, that would be a good life.* Well, the good news is that prayer *is* our job as Christian women. This good life awaits us. The bad news is that our overly busy lives are filled with demands and time-taking responsibilities: caring for the house, supporting our family, and managing our jobs and businesses.

We must make prayer a priority or it will never happen. Prayer must become so important that we are willing to let other important things go undone. It is not a matter of just knowing this truth...we need to make decisions based on prayer's significance. We need to *believe and decide* that our lives are incomplete if we do not spend time praying daily. We need to *believe and decide* that the only way to live a full and rewarding life is to spend time with God in prayer. Think about it. If God—the orchestrator of our ultimate plan—is not leading and directing us, then sooner or later we will be lost and unfulfilled.

There was a time when I worried that even if I found the time for prayer, I would not have enough to pray about. How I underestimated the depth of my spiritual hunger! Once you feast at the table of mercy and grace, you truly long to be fed again. And like a fine, satisfying meal, prayer time has become my daily highlight. These days I yearn to feed on God's Word and hear His word. When I miss my time with Him, I feel scattered from the lack of nourishment.

Dr. Martin Luther King Jr. wrote, "I have to hurry all day long to get time to pray." I am no longer rushing my prayer so I can get to my day. I now have things in the proper order. I am rushing my day to get more time to pray.

God not only tells us it is His desire for us to pray to Him, He tells us why we should pray. In James 5:16 He tells us that "the effective, fervent prayer of a righteous man avails much." When a believer prays, great things happen. When we decide to the use the tool of prayer, God will swing open new doors of opportunity for us, and we will start achieving beyond our wildest imagination. We will walk into places we never thought we would go. He will bring people into our lives to show us how to move to the next level. The power of Ephesians 3:20-21 will open up for us: "Now to Him who is able to do exceedingly abundantly above all that we ask or think, according to the power that works in us, to Him be the glory in the church by Christ Jesus."

I have seen the hand of God move in my life this way. One year after starting my staffing company, I received the opportunity to meet with a Fortune 500 company regarding a 60-million-dollar-a-year contract. When I went to the second meeting to give a presentation, I was alone. And I felt it. I did not have a fancy Power Point presentation or a projector. Armed with just a laptop computer and a presentation I had spent the entire night preparing at a copy center, I drove onto the company's campus. Everything was massive and impressive. The discrepancy between this company's obvious grandness and my apparent insignificance fueled the spirit of fear. It crept into my thoughts and my nervous system and told me I did not have what it takes to present to this company. See how counterproductive fear can be? I worked all night on a project and gave it my best, and I still let fear bully me. But only for a while.

Before I left my car, I prayed down this spirit of fear and asked God to go before me. I asked Him to give me favor with each decision maker. If I had known how to pray then as I do now, I would have asked Him to justify and glorify me—to validate and magnify my offerings. As I walked into the lobby the prayers kept on coming. I asked God to be my ever-present help because I felt a little intimidated. When I arrived at the conference room, I plugged in my laptop, sent up some more prayers, and began the presentation with four people gathered around my little computer screen. Everyone was quiet throughout the entire presentation, which was a bit unnerving, so I prayed without ceasing. At the end of the presentation, the female executive in charge asked me to stay and speak with her privately. Talk about nervous! Here I had prayed the entire time, yet my human nature could not relax and rest in

God's provision. It is a learning process. But what happened next inspired a spiritual growth spurt. The executive looked at me with a strange expression and in absolute silence for what seemed like an eternity. She broke her silence, but the puzzled look on her face remained. "Victoria, I do not know why I am giving you this contract. Your company is only a 10-million-dollar company, and I am giving you a 60-million-dollar contract. All I know is that I am supposed to give you this contract." All I could muster was a very sincere, "If you are supposed to give me this contract, then I pray you will be obedient."

I managed to contain myself until I had thanked her and headed to the lobby. But as soon as I got to the lobby, I ran out of the front doors shouting praises to the one and only true God who had come through for me and cleared the way. Once I had regained my composure, I walked to my car and shouted some more. I saw the hand of God move on that executive's heart and mind right before my eyes. God had given me favor with her in a mighty way. My prayers had been answered.

We must understand that daily prayer is the only way to experience spiritual power, direction, and purpose. By spending meaningful time with God every day, we will receive new power over our circumstances. We no longer have to face life and our troubles without having the power to make the necessary changes. Prayer allows God to open opportunities for you that are bigger than anything you could even think to ask for. Prayer is the answer to living a successful life. Prayer works!

Pray Effectively and Consistently

It deeply concerns me that many women do not feel they know how to pray. I want to tell you that God must have known we would have this problem because He provided a solution for problems that did not exist yet. "Likewise the Spirit also helps us in our weaknesses. For we do not know what we should pray for as we ought, but the Spirit Himself makes intercession for us with groanings which cannot be uttered" (Romans 8:26). God assists those of us who do not know how to pray with assistance from the Holy Spirit. The Holy Spirit intercedes with groaning. This might be a strange idea for our contemporary minds, but think of it as expressing emotion that is so personal, so spiritual, that mere words cannot be used. The Holy Spirit even begs God on our behalf in this deeply intimate, spiritual way. God is not concerned with words, labels, or our self-diagnosis. He is focused on our longings, desires, sighs, and tears. Inward prayer reaches heaven's highest places.

There are times when I have cried out to God with such hurt and disappointment I could not find the words to pray. I could only cry, moan, or hum my prayer. And I know the Holy Spirit has interceded on my behalf.

Have you ever been standing in church singing praise or worship songs, and felt so overwhelmed by pure emotion that all you could do was hum every other chorus? One moment you are lifting your voice and your hands in worship, and the next you can only lift up your brokenness, your hurts, your groanings. This is communion with the Father.

The beauty of praying to God is He is not concerned about us knowing how to pray. He just wants us to get started, and He will assist us once we make the effort. After we invest time praying consistently, we become confident and strong in our prayer life. This only happens by committing to daily prayer and studying the Bible.

The Process of Prayer

When I received my first two-wheel bike, I could not wait to feel the wind in my hair and the freedom of mobility. However, as my eyes dropped to notice how very thin those black tires were, my heart sank as well. When older kids had circled around the neighborhood on their brightly colored bikes, I had not paid attention to the wimpy tires responsible for their speed. Not wanting to appear cowardly, I hopped on the bike and pedaled slowly. Balance did not come easy, and with siblings shouting directions— "Steer with both hands," "Look up," "Keep your feet on the pedals"—this so-called leisurely activity turned into an overwhelming process.

Prayer, a simple act of faith, becomes overwhelming when we do not know what to do with our mind, heart, and bodies while on our knees. *Do I speak? Listen? Fold my hands? Look up or down? Must my eyes be closed? How long does God require me to be still?* So we jump into an awkward prayer or rote commentary that seems identical to our prayer the day before. My bike-riding skills improved once I learned the process and practiced it over and over. Scraped knees, a dented fender, a torn shoe later, and I knew just how to transport myself. I even began to ride fast, around tight corners, and—when Mom wasn't looking—I raised my hands over my head and coasted. Learning the process of prayer and finding a comfortable way to transport ourselves to God's presence is a joy that offers active communication and freedom to move forward in our faith.

If it has been a while since you prayed with your heart or if you have stopped talking to God because a situation of pain or doubt silenced your voice, I invite you to move past your fear, ignore the thin tread lines made from past, weary travels, and get back to it.

If you need a place to start, God gives us a way to tap into the process and passion of prayer. Matthew 6:6-13 teaches us how to pray:

> But you, when you pray, go into your room, and when you have shut your door, pray to your Father who is in the secret place; and your Father who sees in secret will reward you openly. And when you pray, do not use vain repetitions as the heathen do. For they think that they will be heard for their many words. Therefore do not be like them. For your Father knows the things you have need of before you ask Him. In this manner, therefore, pray: Our Father in heaven, hallowed be Your name. Your kingdom come. Your will be done on earth as it is in heaven. Give us this day our daily bread. And forgive us our debts, as we forgive our debtors. And do not lead us into temptation, but deliver us from the evil one. For Yours is the kingdom and the power and the glory forever. Amen.

Since I began cultivating my daily prayer life, I have seen God move in my life in a mighty way. I have gone from fearing what might happen every day to entrusting every moment to His hands. When situations come up in my life, I pray about them and move forward, believing God will handle everything I face.

Principle Prayer

Lord, I have ignored Your call to prayer so many times. I come before You filled with need, hope, and also questions as to how to talk to You. I know You hear this humble prayer and call it good. You desire to have communion with me,

Your creation. How wonderful You are, Lord. Within my spirit is the urge to sit before You in stillness and receive what You have to speak to my heart. I will work on my prayer life, Lord. I commit my time and my open heart to You this week as I learn how to just "be" in Your presence once again. And even though You know what is on my heart, Lord, I look forward to sharing it openly and seeking Your wisdom and love for my life. Amen.

$\mathcal{P}$rinciple in Practice

1. Create a prayer closet in a corner of a room, at a window, or in a special chair.

2. Pray daily and plan for sacrificial time in the morning.

3. Practice listening first.

4. Keep a weekly prayer journal. Write down how God is leading you. List your praises and reflect on them.

5. Select one new Scripture a week to live by and keep in your heart.

6. Pray for someone else every day for one week.

7. Pray over all your decisions (family, work, business, finance, and so on).

$\mathcal{B}$elieve in Your Purpose

Believe God has a plan just for you.
Utilize your unique gifts and talents to fulfill this purpose.

> "And we know that all things work together for
> good to those who love God, to those who are
> called according to His purpose."
>
> ROMANS 8:28

More than 15 years ago, when I faced leaving Chicago to move
to Los Angeles, I knew God was up to something. I had a beautiful apartment, great friends, wonderful business associates, and
had finally found an incredible church and pastor. I was living
only four hours from the home in St. Louis where I grew up. And
I had a great job that I loved. That is, until I was laid off. That
was the beginning of a shift in circumstances that led me to the
West Coast. Looking back now, it is very apparent that God was
forcing me out of my comfort zone.

Because one of my sisters was living in L.A., I had some fun
initially. I enjoyed Southern California's exotic version of winter
as I made plenty of time for driving to the beach, shopping, and

visiting many new restaurants. But when the novelty of constant sunshine grew dim, I felt lonely and lost. I missed my friends and everything that was familiar to me. What was God doing? After being in Los Angeles six months, I began searching for answers. It became clear that He had moved me to a new place... to this place, for His purpose. Now I just needed to figure out what that was exactly. I knew this process could take one day or ten years.

The Path to Discovering Your Purpose

It is so easy to forget that God's purpose for our lives is larger than our plans, feelings, or desires. God's purpose goes far beyond the scope of our current resources or circumstances. The plans God has for us exceed anything we could think or imagine for our lives. We were born by His purpose for His purpose.

To go down God's path, we have to be willing to step out and take a risk. Usually God's purpose requires us to walk by faith and not by sight. This is not easy and most times is not convenient, and usually a sacrifice must be made. Relationships, possessions, and our lifestyles may have to be given up. God is looking for people who are sold out for His purpose, people who are willing to stand tall and do whatever is required to get the job done. He is looking for some spiritual risk takers. People who believe that all the dreams and visions God has revealed are not impossible. They are real, and it is His desire that they come to life. God is working day and night setting us to accomplish our purpose.

God wants us to live happy and fulfilling lives, but at the end of the day it is His agenda that must be driven forward. We must understand that He put a plan together just for you and me. We do not just fall into the roles we play in life. So many of us think we face difficult times because our life situation is all an accident. This is far from the truth. Everything happens for a purpose.

Life Is a Set-Up

God sets us up to meet certain people and make certain things happen at just the right time. A great example of how He works is the life of my dear friend David Perry, who went from being homeless and on drugs to establishing a national photography business in just a couple of years. God sent every resource David needed to establish his business. He first came into contact with the photography business while in the military in Japan. He was looking at a magazine and became curious about how people made money taking pictures. So he bought a camera and began taking pictures for military special occasions and events to gain experience. He became known as the man to go to for pictures.

Once David got out of the military, he attended photography classes and worked to improve his hobby. After so much time of taking pictures for free, a friend paid him 200 dollars to be the photographer at a special event. Suddenly the doors opened up, and so did David's understanding of his purpose. Today he owns a national firm that covers events for major corporations and organizations such as Nike, State Farm Insurance, Urban League, NAACP, and many more.

God sent all the right people, all the necessary resources, and everything David needed to start his business and move forward in a successful life. It was all set up by God.

God has a reason for everything He created. God will release everything you need at an appointed season. He provides the resources, the knowledge, and the power. We often think, "I just happened to meet so and so, and she called so and so, and the next thing I knew I was in business." That isn't what happened at all. When you see God's hand on your life, you are able to believe in your purpose. This principle is essential for you to embrace before you are able to tap into your God-given abilities and follow the vision for your life. Believing that your purpose is designed by God is the catalyst for a successful life.

Getting on Track

How do we know we are off track? At first it just feels like everyday frustration. A deal doesn't go through. You miss an opportunity you should have noticed. Decision making seems clouded by doubt or other barriers. You can glean lessons from these situations, but chances are, you have not stepped in line with God's purpose for your life yet. When you are on the right track, even mistakes can direct you toward your purpose.

It is very exciting to research and uncover what God's plan is for you. There is excitement when you get up in the morning and head toward the day. Your creativity is sparked and your thoughts seem to fall in place for things to be accomplished. When you are on track, you cannot wait to see what will happen next. Even as you face the unknown, there is a security in God's direction. Your prayers of faith lead you toward the next milestone along the journey. We begin to realize we are walking in our purpose with faith backing us up all the way.

You should not live another day without beginning the journey of finding or living in your purpose. You can start by getting in your prayer closet. It must be a place where you can put everything else aside while you focus on your relationship with God. Once you are in your closet, close your eyes and ask God to usher you into His presence. Take your time and inhale and exhale His air. God will begin to provide you with what I call insider information. He pours out answers to cover the questions you have been holding on to for some time. Situations you have been trying to figure out become resolved. All along, God just wanted us to bring our burdens to Him. "The LORD is on my side; I will not fear" (Psalm 118:6).

He wants us to sit down and bring our thoughts and desires to Him. He wants us to stop trying to fix things and put our little bandages on our problems. When we finally turn matters over to Him, He can work in our lives without our interference. Our focus can be on His wonders and His will instead of our problems. There is an interesting phenomenon that takes place when we turn over our lives to God. Our lives can seem laden with even more troubles, as though God is stirring up more trouble, when in reality He is solving our problems and working them out for good. Once you understand how His hand is upon your life and moving through situations, you will race to your prayer closet in anticipation of being in His presence. You will begin to pray for miracles and believe by faith that He will provide them...because you will know what He has done.

Examine Your Life

In discovering our purpose we should look at our lives closely to see who we are and how God made us. Spend time examining your childhood and young adult years. You can learn a lot about your purpose through hindsight. Before adult expectations or troubles started to direct your path, how was God leading your heart? Have you carried over into adulthood the same interests? Did you continue to develop those abilities and nurture those passions imprinted on your spirit?

As you analyze these areas of your life, you should begin to know yourself better. My prayer is that you will start to see your life as God sees it…complete with amazing abilities, uniqueness, and a bright future. Once you get a glimpse of your God-given purpose, the work God is doing will become clear. He is leading you along the path created just for you.

Think through these questions. Or go through them with a friend and have that friend answer on your behalf. You might find her perspective interesting and insightful. Review your answers and see what stands out as *the* something you like to do and that you do well. Become reacquainted with yourself. Look closely at all the things God has allowed you to do. Look back on all the places He has allowed you to go. Whom has God placed along your path? It is wonderful to observe your life. You might be surprised how many strengths and interests you have.

Childhood

- Were you shy and quiet or outspoken and aggressive?
- Were you always busy doing something or were you the kid who stayed in your room reading?
- Did you enjoy playing indoors or outdoors?
- Were you creative and artsy?
- Were you an early riser, or did your parents have to drag you out of bed?

- Was your room clean or messy?

- How did you tackle homework? Did you do it willingly?

- What subjects did you enjoy or excel in at school?

- Among your peers, were you a leader or more of a follower?

Adulthood

- Do you enjoy being around others or being alone?

- What natural gifts and talents seem to serve you best at work and at home?

- What do you enjoy doing? Could those hobbies be more than just hobbies?

- What makes you feel alive and motivated?

- What are you brilliant at?

- What do others compliment you on consistently?

- What do you do that other people marvel at and can't come close to doing?

What you do well and how you choose to use that talent will affect your road to success. In his book *Maximize the Moment*, Bishop T.D. Jakes writes, "You were built with a specific purpose in mind. There is a reason you have the personality that you do. There is a reason that you have the needs and abilities that you have. That doesn't mean that there are not areas in you that require discipline and focus. But I want you to realize that much of what God has endowed you with is neither good nor bad. It is neutral and nebulous until you use it for good or bad."[1]

Stay Focused

The devil will want to lead you from focusing on your strengths and points of brilliance. The longer he can distract you from your purpose, the better for his plan. A way to ensure that you stay focused on your own purpose is to run your own race. Don't take up the race of someone else just because they have found success in some particular area or arena. We think what they are doing looks easy and fun, so we may feel we can do what they are doing. It looks interesting because we have not taken the time to look at God's personal plan for us. We have not planned our own race. If you attempt to run the race of another, you will quickly discover that God packaged each one of us differently.

Keep your eyes on the areas where you shine. And where you are lacking, God is preparing people around you to shine so there will be fruitfulness and wholeness. That is where running your own race becomes essential. You might be designed to help complete part of another person's plan...a part that only you are prepared to do. Others who are abiding by their purpose will rise to meet your needs at a God-appointed time.

"And we know that all things work together for good to those who love God, to those who are called according to His purpose. For whom He foreknew, He also predestined to be conformed to the image of His Son, that He might be the firstborn among many brethren. Moreover whom He predestined, these He also called; whom He called, these He justified; and whom He justified, these He also glorified" (Romans 8:28-30). Not only did He call you, He justified you. He demonstrated or proved you to be just, right, and valid. God has validated your purpose. You do not need validation from your coworkers, neighbors, or peers. God has you covered. Do not get me wrong—it is wonderful to be approved and praised by people, but when God calls you to do something, you have to step past the approval of others and hang on to His word and purpose for your life.

When something seems so beyond your current ability or training, God will take care of that too. He has glorified you. Glorify can mean to give glory, honor, or high praise to, and it also means to cause to be seen more glorious or excellent than is actually the case. Through the lens of faith and purpose, God magnifies your abilities.

The Greek word for "purpose" is *prothesis*. "Pro" means before and "thesis" is a place, thus a setting forth. The word suggests a deliberate plan, a proposition, an advanced plan, an intention, a design. God has a customized plan for you that was made in advance. It is our job to discover and line up with our purpose. God has already put the entire plan together. We just have to walk in it. He did not promise there would not be any battles. There will be battles, but He will handle them. His plan covers every situation you will face. It covers every financial crisis, every heartbreak, every trial. He will give you everything you need to accomplish the task at hand. So when you are not sure you have what it takes, or you don't know if you can make it, remember that believing in your purpose requires admitting you cannot handle it and knowing that God can.

Fill the Void

If we are not lined up with our purpose, there is a deep void in our lives. Joy does not fill us. We cannot see past what is on our plates at the moment to the great things to come. It doesn't matter how much money we make or what status our business card reflects, every day there is something that just doesn't feel right. We struggle to get out of bed. We go to the closet, and even though we just went shopping for something to wear, nothing in the entire closet seems to fit our day. We settle on something and head into the kitchen. The groceries we bought yesterday are not appealing this morning. We settle again or we skip the meal altogether. We rush to get the kids to school and then barely make it to work. Our frustration level is high, and the gray walls at work agitate us. The day drags on, and everyone we interact with seems annoying or incompetent. After work the usual evening plays out. We take care of dinner, homework with the kids, and entertain visions of a long bath and then reading the Bible before bed. The bath and the alone time with God do not happen...again. You fall asleep the moment your head hits the pillow, and soon you are facing the same day all over again.

When did life get this boring? When did the thought of another day become a reason to cry rather than celebrate? If you look back over your life and reflect on the questions we addressed earlier, I think you will discover times when you did rejoice in each new day and its opportunities.

Reclaim that excitement by cherishing the truth of a Father's love. Believe in the plan He has customized for you and your life. I believe God set me up and justified me and then poured His glory over me. I grow excited when I think of how good He is! I get to walk in His justification and glory every day with my head held high. "In Him also we have obtained an inheritance, being predestined according to the purpose of Him who works all things according to the counsel of His will, that we who first trusted in Christ should be to the praise of His glory" (Ephesians 1:11-13). Some people may look at me and say, "She thinks she is somebody." On the inside, I say to myself, "I am somebody. I am a child of the King and have been predestined for greatness."

Everyone reading this book has been created with a purpose that God wants to fulfill. Many of you are well on your way to becoming entrepreneurs, athletes, writers, actors, mothers, fathers, engineers, editors, doctors, architects, film directors, scientists, money managers, preachers, teachers, and many more vibrant, successful roles.

Fill the void with your God-given purpose and move toward the success He has planned for you.

Principle Prayer

Creator of my life and my purpose, I pray for Your hand to guide my days. I explore my life and realize how faithful You are, even when my eyes were set on things of the world. Even when I was reaching for any and every success that appeared before me instead of realizing the success You planned for me. Now I am ready to pare away the distractions and sins and desires that the devil applauds but that are only keeping me away from my purpose. How did I ever question my worth, Lord? I cannot wait to stand tall and walk with faith into what lies ahead. Thank You for knowing me so intimately that You created this miracle of a life just for me. Amen.

*P*rinciple in Practice

1. Take a look at your current circumstances. Is God trying to nudge you out of your comfort zone? Think of a time He has directed you in a new direction, you resisted, and it brought you closer to your purpose.

2. Examine your life, past and present, to discover your natural abilities and to turn your focus on your purpose.

3. Choose three of your strengths and decide how to use each one specifically for good.

4. Are you on or off track? Ask God to guide your heart to move forward.

5. Reclaim the joy of your salvation and renew your passion for God's purpose in your life. Find a way to mark this decision. Write up a covenant agreement between you and God. Sing praises. Tell your friends or mentors so you have accountability. Or get rid of something in your life that has hindered your belief in your purpose.

6. Make one decision each day this week that moves you closer toward your purpose and real success.

PART TWO:
Vision

ℱollow Your Vision

Couple your imagination with God's plan for your life.
See beyond limitations and move forward in His purpose.

> "And it shall come to pass afterward that I will
> pour out My Spirit on all flesh; your sons and
> your daughters shall prophesy, your old men
> shall dream dreams, your young men shall see
> visions."
>
> JOEL 2:28

Intelligent, creative, and hardworking. I could be describing a strong candidate for a job, but sadly I am describing the characteristics possessed by countless men and women who are living unfulfilled lives. Maybe you have joined the ranks of such an unfortunate club. Allow me to take a closer look at your group of malcontents: They have talent, but rather than stretch, they do only the job set before them. They labor to keep the paycheck, not the passion. They work, but they don't know what they are working toward. This is perhaps the easiest life trap to fall into, yet the hardest to climb out of. Why? Because we don't know any better. Scripture warns us, "My people are destroyed for lack of knowledge" (Hosea 4:6). That is a strong warning. People perish for lack of knowledge, lack of understanding, lack of a relationship with God. If you work without a personal vision, you can implement a dozen corporate projects, but your own dreams will remain inactive.

Whether you punch a time clock, stay home to raise your children, or direct a corporation, your sacrifice of time and effort should serve the vision God has given to *you*. Any of these situations might be exactly the right place for you to be, but you won't find your work fulfilling until you discern your purpose and pray for your vision.

Is Your Life Half Fulfilled?

Have you ever spent an afternoon flipping through magazines reflecting on worlds completely different from your own? The glossy pages profile lives filled with excitement or opportunity you thought only existed in novels. Your daydreams let you explore how great it would be to travel, lead a company, serve the poor, run for mayor...CRASH. Your mind runs into a roadblock when the phone rings, the baby cries, or your computer beeps to remind you of a deadline. So you shove the dream aside—not the magazine version—but the one that was beginning to formulate in your own spirit. Of course, you *do* have to go back to your responsibilities; just don't squelch your spirit.

If you felt a spirit-tug when you read about a woman who started an inner-city ministry, that is knowledge about yourself. You experienced a sense of joy because this woman didn't just talk about it...she did it. She left a fancy house in the hills to be in the squalor of the street, but you recognize success when you see it. The strangest things have tugged at my heart. Think about the times you have felt this kind of elation. Chances are, your heart had witnessed an authentic vision.

Vision: Dreams in Action

Vision allows us to put our dreams into action and embrace knowledge about how to live our lives. While purpose is the "why and what" of life, vision is the essential "how." Thankfully, we will never control our total destiny—that is God's job—but through vision we determine the shape our purpose will take. We can question our current circumstance, compare it to the vision, and make plans accordingly. The questions that occupy your mind and heart at this very moment are helping you discover and form your vision. *Should I stay at home and raise my children? Should I go back to school and obtain the degree in marketing I have always wanted? Will I excel in corporate America, or is it time for me to start my own business? Should I start my own ministry, or should I support one of the ministries at my church?*

When Dreams Are Born

The word "destiny" can have a mystical connotation, but when we embrace destiny as God's plan for our lives, it is a practical spiritual goal. Once developed, our vision leads us to a step-by-step process for achieving our dreams. I will never forget how I felt when I discovered my vision. Successfully employed with a national staffing company in California, I had enjoyed the corporate climb from sales representative to regional manger. But after eight years, I noticed some classic symptoms: restlessness, frustration, boredom. Diagnosis: Unfulfilled. Every morning I had to force myself out of bed and in to the office. I confess I was so restless I sought any reason to take a day off work. I desperately felt the need for change...to move forward somehow. You see? My entire being knew I had traded my personal vision for the job's vision. I was on my way to an unhappy life if I did not start paying attention.

This professional lull paralleled a personal pull to have a child. My husband and I decided to start trying before I made any further career decisions. To our surprise and delight, we became pregnant three months later. I could ignore my spiritual restlessness because my attention shifted to the wonder of future parenthood. I thanked God for His impeccable timing and went about the business of life feeling blessed and secure in my future.

God, however, had other plans.

During my pregnancy I went into prelabor and had to be rushed to the hospital. Talk about spiritual whiplash: One minute I am praising God for His perfect plan and the next minute I am asking Him to save the child in my womb. I did not understand why we were facing such a trial. Lying on a narrow bed, I gazed straight up, not wanting to see the look of concern on the nurse's face. I counted ceiling tiles and tried to ignore the monitors measuring my breath, my pulse, and my baby's chance for survival. Doctors did their best to control a situation that was beginning to feel out of control. Nobody could stop the labor pains or my tears. It was then that I turned to the only help I had—God.

Even with a heart full of questions I believed He was in control. I prayed for God to save my child and give me another chance to be the woman He had designed me to be. I made promises and tried to make deals. If He saved our baby I would serve Him the rest of my life. I would be available and obedient to whatever He wanted me to do.

During this time of my life I was a Christian, but I was not walking with God on a daily basis. I had slipped into a life of convenient commitment—walking with Him on Sunday and being a good person Monday through Saturday. Though I don't think God is in the business of making deals, I do believe He honored my decision to turn to Him rather than away from Him. And He showed up that day in the hospital.

I know what you are thinking...lots of medication, a highly stressful situation...but this was not a hallucination. In fact, nothing has ever been more real. God made His presence known to me in that moment, in that sterile hospital room. Like a father at the sickbed of his child, God told me everything would be all right. He told me the baby would survive. In fact, the message I was getting from God was, "This is not about the baby; she will be fine. This is about you and me, missy." And as the fears for my baby's well-being subsided, God revealed that He had very specific work for me to do after the baby was born—work that would lead me into a season of great success followed by ministry.

After spending five days in the hospital, the labor ceased, and I was sent home to spend the remainder of my pregnancy on bed rest. Ironically, after all those days of wishing for a reason to stay home from my job, I now spent hours, days, and weeks dreaming of being productive, busy, and back at work. But this baby meant everything to me, so I put my hyper personality on pause and rested in God's mercy. In February I delivered a healthy little girl. Each time I held my sweet baby, Briana, I was holding proof of God's word to me that day in the hospital. In my heart I knew His promise of specific work and success would unfold as well. With deep gratitude, I waited for the next step.

When God Says "Now"

As God would have it, I would not wait long. During my days of stillness and deep prayer, God had directed my thoughts toward the idea of owning my own staffing company. Once Briana was born, God confirmed He would bless me with such a business. I was thrilled—and quite surprised that this significant change was meant to happen immediately. I could hear the worry in my mother's voice over the phone when I explained all the things God was telling me to do. She was wondering what happened to her typically rational daughter, the stable child who planned every move with painstaking care. Leaving my job and building a business right after having a baby seemed far from normal. But man's timing and God's timing are rarely the same. And I had promised to follow God.

So, I got busy. I chose the company name, set up the bank accounts, and did everything I could do from home. When Briana turned three months old, I officially started my business from my living room. Joined by one unpaid, faithful employee, Carin, who became my partner, I worked diligently at organizing files, developing contacts, and putting the concept into action. Even as I labored so hard to set the business on a course for achievement, God cautioned me to not get caught up in the future success of this particular company; He was only creating it to give me a platform for ministry. Now, ministry might scare away a lot of folks, but at this time in my life and with everything God had placed on my heart in a few short months, I did not question the idea of ministry. I did, however, question why He did not just send me to seminary and allow the ministry to get started (evidence that the rational part of me was alive and well).

You will discover that in God's perfect will for your life there are no shortcuts. My faith was zealous but still a bit naïve. God was not just calling me to minister and generate a path among Christians, He wanted me to first establish successful relationships with all of His children. The business being formed in my living room was tied to a vision bigger than I could imagine at that time. I considered myself to be a bright woman, but I was not smart enough to develop such a wonderful, comprehensive plan for my life. God was preparing me to have a testimony. God wanted my success—and path to that success—to help build the kingdom. He was preparing to do a new thing in my life.

One of my life inspirations is Harriet Tubman. Her struggle to lead slaves to freedom is celebrated and told as a story of great personal sacrifice. But an amazing truth about Harriet is that this woman of courage and vision was mentally ill from years of physical abuse at the hand of her slave master. The woman responsible for saving countless lives was *mentally ill.* Now, I was pretty sure my publisher would not let me get away with listing "Mental Illness" as a spiritual principle, but the truth is that God might ask you to put aside "normal" or "rational" thinking so you can take on His knowledge and realize your vision. Sometimes you have to think differently to gain courage and be open to God's call.

Life Beyond the Rut

Life can take over even the best intentions and the best dreams. The years pass by before we get the chance to accomplish many of the goals we have been praying and dreaming about since childhood. It is very easy to replace dreaming and planning with maintaining. Even if we are unintentionally embracing "getting by" instead of "moving forward," we undermine our belief that dreams really can come true. We have squelched the spirit too many times.

No wonder the dreaded "rut" we all refer to takes the breath and energy out of us like a sickness. Depression can set in, and we stop looking forward to the days ahead. *Why bother...those days will look exactly like this one.* As our aspirations make an exit, negativity enters our attitudes, decisions, relationships, and thoughts. When sarcasm and doubt become our first reaction to any situation, I call this "stinking thinking." The possibility of living out our dreams seems impossible. Instead of determining a path forward and taking control of the steps of progress, we settle for wherever life or other people's choices takes us. Then we wonder why we are not satisfied with the journey or the destination.

Okay, I had to point out the downside of the rut before I could direct you toward the upside of a purpose- and vision-oriented life. Let's get a bird's-eye view of your current circumstance. Perch on a limb above your current circumstances to see how you got to the rut. Look at how your times of decision and indecision created a path leading right to the entrance of those trenches. Change begins with wisdom and vision. Stay on that limb for a bit longer. I want you to explore your life and personal vision from this vantage point. I am sure you could use a vacation from the rut. Am I right?

Give Time to the Dream

Have you taken the time to sit down and determine what your dreams and goals are? Now is a great time. Grab a notebook, a journal, or just a quiet corner and respond to the following questions. Sift through any initial negative responses (such as, "I should have done *that* five years ago"), and let your heart speak to you. Invite God to join you for this time of exploration.

- What do you want to accomplish in life?
- Are you on track with where you want to be? How do you know?
- What do you want out of life?

- Where do you want to go?
- Whom do you want to meet?
- What do you long to see?

Don't give up on your dreams, friend. "You only have one life to live." You hear it from the pulpit, you hear it from elderly relatives, you whisper it to yourself when you are alone, but let today be the time you take heed of this truth. We have more than an earth-bound life; as Christians we have our sights on eternity. Plant a seed for your dream today and watch it grow toward heaven.

The Seeds of a Dream

I was fortunate to grow up in an entrepreneurial family. As I watched my mom and dad run their business, I longed to do the same some day. The seeds of a dream were planted. I imagined myself walking into an office knowing it was my company and the result of hard work and strong faith. As a young girl, I would wake up in the middle of a dream with ideas about my future business. I began writing down important details so they would not disappear in the haze of morning. What is it about God and sleepless nights? I think our spirits truly seek God and His guidance during our sleeping hours. For one thing, it is probably the only time God can get a word in edgewise.

My parents never had a regular paycheck or a nine-to-five job. They owned a large construction and excavation company. I watched them drive trucks, tractors, and trailers as they built freeways, overpasses, and roadways. Each day they had to make it happen for themselves. Even at the age of seven I recognized how much work, public relations, and marketing it took just to get a job. My folks had to overcome added obstacles because they were among very few African-American business owners in their industry. Yet they kept the work flow coming. Entrepreneurship made an impression that would last a lifetime and become a part of my vision.

Do you dream big dreams or little ones? Are you expecting God to do a little through you, or are you expecting Him to do great, spectacular things through you? We serve a big God who transformed the dark of nothingness into the color of heaven and earth. And yet many of us still want more proof. Goodness, we are a tough jury, are we not? We serve a God who hung the stars and clouds in the sky and told them to stay there. Yet we question where God has placed us. We pray to a God who envisioned intricate designs for the oceans, flowers, and animals. Yet we question our own value and uniqueness. We bow down to a God who used dust and dirt to shape a man and then breathed life into that form. Yet we use our precious breath to curse our circumstances rather than praise God for our many blessings. We serve a God who has all power in His hand. Yet we place our limited idea of Him in a little box.

The true God, the mighty Lord, the loving Creator will take our dreams in His hand and blow His breath into them to bring our purpose to life. God's Word tells us, "Now to Him who is able to do exceedingly abundantly above all that we ask or think, according to the power that works in us, to Him be glory in the church by Christ Jesus" (Ephesians 3:20-21). Do not follow God's power and promises with another "yet" statement. Do not exchange God's intended purpose for a list of "but I can't" rebuttals. God wants to do more for us than we can ask for or imagine. These verses tell me God is passionate about blessing us. Are you passionate about becoming successful?

Passionate Commitment

Let's look at a selection of visions that occupy some women's spirits and hearts. Consider the passion, talents, and motivation that might light a fire under each of these unique visions.

- "I plan to help my community by becoming involved and leading."
- "I want to work from home while my children are young."
- "I'm ready to start a novel. I think I have a good idea for a story."
- "I want to develop a business that provides a creative environment for employees and clients."
- "I want to work my way up to management in a solid, ethical company."

Passion can be equated with powerful emotions such as love, joy, hatred, or anger. Passion is boundless enthusiasm. What are you passionate about? Through my experiences I have found that passion alone is not enough. We must also be committed to our plans and goals. Commitment means to be bound emotionally or intellectually to someone or something. When we put passion and commitment together, we have a special recipe that creates a unique life direction. Passionate commitment gives us a game plan that becomes unstoppable.

When we are passionately committed to something, our behavior changes. Passion inspires us to reach further and excel, while commitment will keep us doing the job even when we are tired or frustrated, or want to give up. Where there is passion, commitment can follow.

What are you passionately committed to? Health care, children, education, clothing, the environment? Determine what is important to you and what you enjoy doing. A dream without passionate commitment is a dream without wings.

Commitment requires dedication to finish what you start. Anyone can start something, but it takes a committed person to complete the task at hand. Dr. Martin Luther King Jr. once said, "If a man hasn't discovered something that he is willing to die for, he isn't fit to live." Have you discovered your "something"?

Passionate commitment is very personal. If you succeed, your confidence and sense of purpose soars. But if you fall short of passionate commitment and haphazardly pursue tasks and objectives, you will not reach your goals. And believe me, this failure and those that are likely to follow become very personal. A little mental tally sheet keeps reminding us of the score. Six failed attempts—zero successes. Seven failed attempts—zero successes. Slowly our self-worth and self-confidence suffer. Others might lose faith in us, but that consequence will never harm us as much as a loss of faith in ourselves. Before we know it, the sin of envy has come to visit and we compare ourselves to everyone around us. Never mind that they are likely having the same inner struggles. All we can see is their apparent success or the chasm between what they have and what we have not. The cycle of defeat pulls us under.

Pursuing your vision and living a fulfilled life are worth the fight. Ecclesiastes 9:10 tells us, "Whatever your hand finds to do, do it with your might." We must choose to fight and push our way through. Just as I had to fight the urge to push during prelabor, there are times we have to be still and wait on God. Then there are circumstances when God says the time is now to push through the pain to the other side. There are moments when pushing and struggling are the only ways to move toward the life God purposed for you. Don't give up. Embrace your vision starting today.

Set a Vision in Motion

Develop a Vision Statement

A vision remains just a wonderful idea until we bring it to life. A plan must be put into place for this to happen. A step-by-step process provides a road map to launch the vision into the realm of reality. A successful plan begins with a vision statement that clearly defines what we are trying to accomplish. Keep it concise so it remains an easy focal point to keep your eyes on the prize and your steps on track. A vision statement contains the following information:

1. Mission Statement: How you plan to accomplish the vision

   Often a mission statement succinctly clarifies who you are, what you do, who you serve, and what makes you unique.

2. Purpose: Why you are accomplishing the vision

3. Goals: Detailed steps to accomplish the vision

A vision statement designed for personal and professional success makes the most of your talents and resources. If your dream includes a business, be sure you begin that process with a corporate vision statement so that you, your business partners, and teammates are all serving the same ultimate goal. More than one vision leads to confusion and makes success impossible.

Nurture the Spirit of Excellence

Excellence is not perfection. I want to state that right up front because there are too many of us striving to be perfect...and breaking our backs and spirits in the process. Don't mistake the impossible, elusive quest for perfection with the achievable, attainable spirit of excellence.

In everything you do and pursue, strive to be *your* best, do *your* best, and live *your* best. Did you notice the emphasis on "your"? The spirit of excellence supports your personal vision and goals. It is not about always being the best or number one...it is about being and doing *your* best in any given situation. In his book *The Greatest Salesman in the World*, Og Mandino writes, "In setting my goals I will consider my best performance of the past and multiply it a hundredfold. This will be the standard by which I will live in the future."[1]

The result of excellence in action for your friend or coworker will look different from your version of excellence. As an individual created with unique abilities, you will approach projects, goals, and the fulfillment of your vision with unique standards. When you start giving your all and doing your very best at all times, people notice, and they will jump at the chance to support your vision. Your extra effort, the way you relate to people, the style in which you present information...whatever you do will make an impression on others. Living with a spirit of excellence will honor God and help you better understand and fulfill your purpose and your vision. Don't ever confuse lack of effort with inability, because you will miss the wonderful gift of discerning your natural abilities. When you strive for excellence, your strengths will rise to the top like cream.

Make the Most of Your Talents and Resources

Our true vision will be in sync with our personality, experiences, natural gifts, and talents. If your vision includes participating in a shuttle run for NASA, but you have a fear of heights and are a homebody who failed science class, then you might want to evaluate that vision. We must look into our collection of personal tools and preferences and determine what we have available to us. An important point here: You might have talents you have not yet tapped into. That is why you go back to the chapter on purpose again and again to determine your strengths.

"There are diversities of gifts, but the same Spirit. There are differences of ministries, but the same Lord. And there are diversities of activities, but it is the same God who works all in all" (1 Corinthians 12:4-6). Your unique talents are given to you by the Lord of all. When you understand your gifts, you can appreciate how special you are. I suggest you use a very business-oriented approach for personal or business ability assessment—identify your hard and soft skills. An example of a hard skill is: "I have three years experience as a graphic artist," or "I have a degree in electrical engineering." A soft skill would be: "I work well in hectic environments," or "I work best in small offices with only a few people." Make a list for both of these categories. You will be surprised by how many you come up with. Ask friends for their input as well.

Once you know your skills and natural abilities, it is important to update and refine them. Updating your skills by taking classes, reading books, or engaging in conversation with those who use the same skills successfully will allow you to keep up with the changing world. Our vision should always be evolving to make the most of our resources. But the abundance or lack of resources should not ever dictate our vision.

Human Resources

Let's organize our resources. In addition to your personal abilities, you are surrounded by people who know people. Think of them as your personal human resources team. Write down categories that are of use to your vision and then seek out those people who can provide assistance in that area. For example, if you are looking for a job, organize your resources in the following categories:

- resume assistance
- reference assistance
- job referrals
- recruiters
- human resource contacts

Our resources are very important because they give us additional knowledge and information that can be transformed into the power we need to make things happen.

Measure Your Progress

It is critical to measure our progress along the way. If we are not keeping track, we will suddenly find ourselves staring at those familiar cavernous walls of the rut and thinking, "How did I get back here?" Measuring progress is key to developing milestones within the plan so we can have mile markers to look for along the way. If you are a jogger or have attempted to start up that habit, you know how important those milestones are to your success and sanity. *I just have to make it to that mailbox up ahead. Just one more round of this track and I am done.*

Once "vision living" becomes second nature, your communication with God and your sense of your spirit's leaning will help you measure how you are doing. To get yourself started, use the goals you listed for the vision statement. (These will change as you see what works and what doesn't, but if you find yourself drastically changing your goals, it might be time to evaluate the original vision statement.) Take those goals and place them in order of logical achievement or helpfulness. Does your number five goal depend on goals three and four to be completed first? Which goals require the help of those resources you listed? And so on. Spend time examining and memorizing your goals. Start your days by reviewing the next few on your list. They will keep your steps heading for success and provide markers along the journey.

Celebrate small successes along the way. You should rejoice in every step you take toward your vision. The end vision could take years to roll out. God might call you on many journeys in between while asking you to remain faithful to the same vision. Because we are human beings who need gratification and assurance, these small and not-so-small victories add up to motivation and inspiration to continue.

Make Adjustments to the Plan

Delays and detours are a part of the driving experience in the Los Angeles area. I have dealt with urban traffic in the Midwest and on the East Coast, but L.A. is in a league all its own. Now that I have grown accustomed to the chaos, I know some secrets to get to business meetings and appointments. I give myself extra driving time. I know alternate routes to my usual destinations. And when I can control the timing of appointments, I plan around rush hours.

Expect delays and detours to be a part of the journey toward your vision. A change in your family situation. Corporate restructuring. Economic shifts. New knowledge that affects your goals. Even welcome opportunities can require us to change our plans.

Follow my driving rules to help you stay flexible in the pursuit of your vision:

- Allow yourself extra time to reach the tougher goals.

- List some alternate resources in case you need more information and contacts along the way. When you meet with one person, always ask them who else might be helpful to speak with. Soon you will have a lengthy alternate list.

- Look ahead and plan around possible obstacles. If financing will arise as a problem, start to research funding right away. Work trouble shooting into your goal setting.

Identify the Barriers

We must look deep within ourselves and determine what is keeping us from accomplishing our dreams. There are so many outside obstacles to watch for, we don't want to be held back by internal struggles as well. The devil is watching and studying us to see what he can use against us. What trick is the devil using to keep you from living the successful life God had in mind when He created you? Is it the neighborhood you grew up in or the way you feel about yourself? Many of us struggle with low self-esteem due to negative childhood experiences or because of our weight, appearance, social status, or education. We feel we do not have what it takes to accomplish the dream that is locked inside of us. What is holding you back?

As I travel around the country, I talk to many women who have put their dreams on a closet shelf and closed the door because life is too hard. There is too much drama. The distance between these women and their dreams becomes so significant they wonder if the dream still exists. Once in awhile, for inspiration, they might sneak a peek at the dream as they reach for a fresh towel or their winter coat. But eventually the sight of that unfulfilled dream will become too painful. This is a tragedy. And it is caused by fear or misleading self-talk that says we do not have what it takes to bring that dream out of the closet and into the light of reality.

I want you to be encouraged. You have everything you require to accomplish your dreams. God deposited everything you need inside your heart and spirit. You are walking around with the seeds of God's purpose already inside of you. That is power. If you feel inadequate or unable, you are listening to the deceiver rather than to the God who does not make mistakes. "For you created my inmost being; you knit me together in my mother's womb. I praise you because I am fearfully and wonderfully made; your works are wonderful, I know that full well" (Psalm 139:13-14 NIV). God made you and your dreams. Know this full well!

I like to ask successful men and women how they dealt with their problems and weaknesses. Not one of them has said, "Oh, Victoria, I didn't have any challenges." Instead, I hear story after story of perseverance, overcoming obstacles, and keeping the vision alive. These men and women have a sense of urgency about life. They understand the importance of family, friends, faith, and time. They receive each day as a gift; therefore, they don't want to waste a minute.

We must make a decision today. We must decide whether we will continue to allow our troubles and weaknesses to deter us from our dreams or will we make up our minds that nothing is going to keep us from a successful life. I hope and pray that the choice you make is to grab your dreams and live life to the fullest and never give up, no matter what obstacles are thrown in your path.

Principle Prayer

Dear Lord, help me reach beyond my insecurities and lay claim to the dream You have planted inside of me. Let me strive to always do my best so that I am honorable and faithful in my actions. Help me to understand, nurture, and use my abilities to follow the vision You have entrusted to me. Thank You for today. It is a gift You give to me—may I give it back to You by pressing forward in Your will. Amen.

*P*rinciple in Practice

1. Determine what you are passionately committed to doing and becoming.

2. Develop a personal and professional vision statement.

3. Decide what "spirit of excellence" means for you.

4. Pray for God to show you what stands between you and your dreams.

5. Assess and update your skills. Sign up for a class or seminar to enhance a skill.

6. Consider how making the vision a reality will align you with your purpose in life.

*M*odel Integrity

Consistently stand for what you believe
and follow through with what you say.

"The integrity of the upright will guide them."
PROVERBS 11:3

It's a typical day. Sheila arises, looks out the window, scratches her head in amazement at how fast the weekend went, and opens her closet. After just moments of deliberation, her decision comes down to the burgundy suit or the yellow cardigan with a navy skirt. Breakfast sounds good but time is limited, so she decides coffee and a pastry will be the breakfast of this champion. Her favorite corner coffee shop is too crowded, so she goes to the one down the street. While standing in line, Sheila contemplates the display of rolls and scones and mentally creates a priority list for the day. She decides to put off writing her assistant's review so she can meet with her supervisor and discuss some great ideas she came up with over the weekend. She can ask for an extension on the review during that meeting. Finally, she faces the barista and asks for a large skim vanilla latte and two chocolate dipped biscotti biscuits to go...one is for her assistant, who loves chocolate. She grabs a copy of the local paper and pays in change.

Decisions fill your every waking moment. You can probably relate to the above scenario of multitasking while merely heading in to the office. *What in the world does choosing biscotti over a maple scone have to do with integrity?* Good question. I wanted to show you how easily we slip in and out of choices throughout our day. Goodness, this scene isn't that much time out of a hypothetical morning, yet it is filled with small and big decisions. And yes, even one that involves integrity. Paying a bill of $8.75 in quarters will bother the four people in line behind Sheila, but that is an issue of courtesy, not integrity. Changing coffee shops won't impact who Sheila is or her vision for success. However, in that blur of choices she made the decision to delay her assistant's review. What if that review was already late? What if Sheila's supervisor had asked her to be on time because the assistant was up for a raise?

Aha. An integrity decision did arise. Sheila was on a decision-making roll. And while it was sweet of her to grab biscotti for her chocolate-loving assistant, I would bet the assistant would prefer to have her salary increase go through. In this imagined vignette, Sheila is so busy making quick choices she does not realize she is putting her integrity on the line with one of those seemingly simple decisions. Not only could her choice undermine her integrity with her staff, it will likely affect her integrity with her supervisor. A boss loves an employee who brings in ideas from a weekend of brainstorming, but she will not receive those ideas unless a foundation of respect is maintained. Sheila possibly placed her own personal vision of success at risk.

Integrity Is a Daily Choice

Real success requires integrity. It is the principle that keeps us grounded. Put wings on those dreams, friend, but keep your feet flat on the touchstone of integrity. It is also the principle that keeps us focused on who we are so we can keep moving in the right direction. When I was growing up in St. Louis, Missouri, my mother and father would always tell my two sisters and me that we had to grow up to be women of integrity so people would respect us and understand just by our character that there were things we would not do. My parents knew the challenges we would face as young women and later as adult women. I think about how many growing girls never hear the word integrity used in relation to their lives. Integrity becomes the basis for confidence, values, and faith. No wonder many young women do not understand their own value.

Respect is earned, not given. Through words, actions, and follow-through people know who we are and who we are not. Women of integrity can be singled out by the way we dress, the manner in which we carry ourselves, how we treat people, our belief system, and the things we choose to participate in and invest our time in. When I think of people with integrity I think of people like Shirley Chisholm, Dr. Martin Luther King Jr., Bishop T.D. Jakes, Colin Powell, my mother, and Eleanor Roosevelt. In fact, I surround myself with the influence of these folks and others. In my office I created what I call my "Inspiration Wall." Framed images of people I admire, respect, and hope to model fill one side of the room. It isn't fancy. It isn't meant to impress people. It is for my eyes only. Each photograph or quote that I post in that space reminds me of honesty, trustworthiness, dependability, strength, proven work ethic, self-confidence, and honor. These are characteristics people of integrity possess and exemplify at all times.

Integrity means to be steadfast. Unmovable. But first we must know what we believe so we can stand firm. This goes back to knowing who we are and who we are not. We need to know where we stand on issues of importance, or others will start telling us what we should think. "The integrity of the upright guides them, but the unfaithful are destroyed by their duplicity" (Proverbs 11:3 NIV).

People of integrity are informed and make informed decisions so they can stand by them. I think as women of faith this notion should be familiar. Our strong faith did not happen because someone else said, "You have to believe this." I grew up in a household where unfortunately this was the mindset. And while I absorbed some good things from the force-fed beliefs of my father, I never could translate those beliefs into an authentic faith for my life. His truth was grounded in perceptions, interpretations, and actions I could not accept as the *absolute* truth. Later I understood his teachings did not fully line up with God's truth. This insight could only take place once I made the effort to study Christianity, embrace truth, grow spiritually, and accept Jesus Christ as my personal Savior.

In the Know

Staying informed has played a key role in my overall success. I take the time to read newspapers, trade publications, and a variety of books so I can interject informed comments during conversations that pertain to business, sports, the environment, government, healthcare, and other topics. There is value in being able to walk into a meeting or reception and contribute my thoughts and perspective.

If you are in the business world, you will find being informed to be helpful when you work with or among men. They can often leave women out of the conversation by assuming we will not be interested in what they are discussing. While that response, in part, relates to their misconceptions, it can also be attributed to their past encounters with women who choose not to be a part of a discussion when men are present. "For God did not give us a spirit of timidity, but a spirit of power, of love and of self-discipline" (2 Timothy 1:7 NIV). It is rewarding to step into a new situation and earn the respect of others.

The Cost of Integrity

Making good decisions is very important. We can look back over our lives and point out many wrong decisions because we tend to obsess over our failures. But think about the good decisions you have made. They reflect strength in your character and moments in your personal journey when you sparkled with integrity. Good decisions are the direct result of choosing to do the right thing. When you unite a clear sense of your vision with a strong character, you are able to discern when a decision or an opportunity is right for your personal journey.

Several years ago a corporation approached me about buying into my company. They wanted to invest a large amount of capital so we could take the company international. At first the offer sounded intriguing. I must admit I started to think about how the money could help with new ventures and add good things to my life and my business. But as the negotiation discussions continued, it became clear that the other company's intentions were not pure. Following my rule of thumb about always being informed, I gathered and assessed all the information I could find on this company. It didn't take long to understand that this company was in pursuit of our minority/woman-owned status only to get the green light for special contracts. To meet the criteria for these opportunities, a minority woman has to control and manage the day-to-day operations of the company. Their plan was to take over the operations while using me and my reputation as the public presence. In other words, I would be allowing them to run what is called a "front." Nobody would have to know.

But I would know.

My integrity kicked in. I saw myself walking around my community pretending to be the owner and operator of a business I was not actually running. Yet I would have walked across stages to receive awards and accolades. I would have spoken to organizations and conference crowds. And with each handshake I would have been implying…and lying…about being an active operator of the business.

Thanks to Mom and Dad, I know who I am and what I stand for. The decision had to be "no deal." I could have sat back and collected the money and used it for good. But my integrity would have suffered great damage. And in the long run, that self-disappointment would have destroyed my chance to fulfill my vision and purpose.

There is not enough money in the world to cover the cost of damages incurred by pretending to be someone you are not. If you start acting a part in order to please someone else or to maintain a level of false importance, you will walk around in fear of being found out. Around every corner there may be someone who could call your bluff, reveal your secret, remove your mask. Pretty soon you lose sight of who you are and who you serve.

I have seen women walk away from their faith out of shame that grew from one bad decision. You are a woman of integrity.

Do not lose yourself in order to achieve what the world defines as success or to resemble what the world says achievement looks like. Hold on to integrity and hold on to your ultimate identity as a child of God. In her book *Jesus, Entrepreneur,* Laurie Beth Jones describes why knowing ourselves is vital to our vision. "I have come to believe that we now must be born three times—once to the world, once to God, and once to ourselves. Because only when we can see who we are and what we stand for—what we want to be about in the world—does every action we take suddenly seem significant. That is the point at which we have realized a vision of ourselves and our path through this world—a path that defines true success."[1]

A Life Examined

God allowed Satan to test Job's integrity because He knew His loving servant would hold on to integrity. The Creator even referred to Job as a man who was "blameless and upright, and one who feared God and shunned evil" (Job 1:1). Integrity was so important, God wanted Satan to see that Job would be faithful even when the pressure was on. In Job 1:11, Satan tells God, "But now, stretch out Your hand and touch all that he has, and he will surely curse You to Your face." So God allowed Satan to attack all of Job's possessions. A messenger informs Job the oxen and donkeys have been taken away during a raid by the Sabeans and his servants have been killed. While Job is speaking to the first messenger another arrives and then another and another. Each with more horrible news. The final messenger reveals that Job's children have been killed during a windstorm. I don't know about you, but after those first couple of messengers shared their sad news I would have hung my "no solicitors" sign on the door and headed for a dark corner.

Can you imagine losing your children and everything you have? How would you respond? I am intrigued and amazed by Job's response. "Then Job arose, tore his robe, and shaved his head; and he fell to the ground and worshiped. And he said: 'Naked I came from my mother's womb, and naked shall I return there. The LORD gave, and the LORD has taken away; blessed be the name of the LORD'" (Job 1:20-21).

Are you crazy, Job? You face one devastating blow after another, all before breakfast, and you choose to bless the name of the Lord? That doesn't quite seem like a measured response to such hardship. Was he in shock? No. He was a man of integrity who was willing to pay the cost in order to preserve that integrity and his faith.

Job's attitude spurned Satan on. His paraphrased response in Job 2:4 is, "Sure, take away his loved ones and his possessions, but all men crumble when their own life is on the line." Had Satan started this betting game with another subject, he might have been right. But God knew Job's heart. He allowed Satan to attack Job's body with the condition that he would not kill Job. Satan struck Job's body with painful boils from the soles of his feet to the crown of his head. Job's wife suggested that he curse God and die. But Job countered with, "'Shall we indeed accept good from God, and shall we not accept adversity?' In all this, Job did not sin with his lips" (Job 2:10). Job would rather die with his integrity than live and curse the God he loved.

God later blessed Job with twice as much as he had lost. He allowed Job to live until he was 140 years old and had seen four generations of grandchildren. He was a blessed man of integrity. We all breathe a sigh of relief when we read about the season of great things in Job's life. These days, we are only comfortable with

Hollywood endings. And yet it is important to understand that the lesson here is not about doing the right thing so you will receive a big payoff. You do not know what the future holds. Job did not know what the future held. He faced loss and death, but he did not swerve from his beliefs. This is integrity.

We too can respond as servants of the Redeemer. As we walk through life, forks in the road appear along the way. Let us carefully, faithfully take the path of integrity which requires us to do the right thing and trust God to take care of us all.

Don't Go There

Before you write off the integrity path because it resembles a road requiring perfection, recall the "spirit of excellence" I shared earlier. Setting a higher life standard does not require perfection. If it did, we would always fall short because we are not called to this goal. Jesus is perfect on our behalf. "Let us fix our eyes on Jesus, the author and perfecter of our faith," (Hebrews 12:2 NIV).

God not only tolerates us, He loves us, in spite of our imperfections. "But God demonstrates His own love toward us, in that while we were still sinners, Christ died for us" (Roman 5:8). While we were imperfect sinners God sacrificed His Son so our sins would be forgiven. Because God has filled the job of Perfect, humans need not apply. Don't go there. Understand the miracle and wonder of grace. And yet, even though I am no longer striving for perfection, I am striving to do my best. I understand now that my goal is to do everything with excellence. "He who has begun a good work in you will complete it until the day of Jesus Christ" (Philippians 1:6). The work God is completing in us is a work of excellence.

Four Kinds of Trust

With the amazing popularity of reality shows on television, millions of viewers are buying into the idea that reality means backstabbing, espionage, lying, cheating, and embracing a dog-eat-dog mentality. That is not reality. Even if these shows are your preferred mind candy, don't accept this anything-for-ratings version of life as your reality. We have all experienced the wrath of people who embrace such tactics. It is difficult to not respond in kind. But before you do, understand that the fork in the road has a little sign which reads "Anything to get ahead...that way. Integrity and trust...this way." The work of excellence God is doing in your life is found along the way of integrity and trust only. Let's explore how the four ways of trust merge with your path to success.

Trust in Yourself

To pursue our vision we must trust ourselves. Many people run the course of their lives never fully trusting themselves to make a decision, do what is right, or achieve a dream. I would bet that right now there is something you are holding back from yourself. It sounds silly, but we all do this until we truly understand who we are, what we stand for, and what we want out of life. This requires some homework and effort. Spend time getting to know what you enjoy and what you are about.

Start by choosing a special place in your home or a favorite café to sit down and finish or review your vision statement. Rediscover and confirm what is important to you and what you stand for. You might have to dig. Sometimes the expectations of others and even past expectations we held for ourselves can override the true vision brewing within our souls. Maybe your impression of yourself is tainted by images of a model in a recent magazine issue, a coworker who wears the best suits, a mother who makes dried flower arrangements to raise money for the poor. For some reason we tend to think whatever she has (whoever *she* is) and however she looks is better than what we have or how we look. When we copy or covet someone else instead of taking the time to figure out what is best for us, that personal journey becomes confusing. Self-doubting has become a favorite pastime for women. But a little love and faith can change that. Pure self-trust begins when we love ourselves.

Love Yourself

You are beautiful. Don't start fidgeting and listing all the things you don't like about yourself. You are beautiful. If you feel the urge to work on a few traits that bother you...so be it. But while you are exercising, coloring your hair, or changing your diet, you must love yourself now or you will never really love the new and improved version.

So spend time today getting to know and love yourself. Compliment five things you have done. Tend to your spirit. Shower yourself with affection by reading God's Word and filling the empty places with abundant goodness. To be whole, healthy, and prepared to live fully, you must embrace all of you—flaws, abilities, brokenness, and quirks. This is love. And even if you never received this kind of love growing up or in your adult life, you still know what it looks and feels like. You are embraced by a Savior's love. "Now hope does not disappoint, because the love of God has been poured out in our hearts by the Holy Spirit who was given to us" (Romans 5:5).

Speak Up for Yourself

If you have ever traveled to a foreign country where you didn't understand the language, you know what it is like to have someone else speak for you. Maybe another tourist on the train took pity on you and asked a local for directions to your hotel. Or a waiter ordered for you after you failed to spit out one discernible word. When you turn over your ability to speak to another person, it is a very unsettling feeling. You lose a bit of yourself and your strength when this sacrifice takes place. The foreign country scenario is a vacation memory to laugh about. But if you frequently end up in situations where others speak for you—in your own language—you lose faith in your own voice and opinion.

Speaking up for ourselves does not require us to be loud and unruly. Loud voices tend to draw attention, but they don't always speak the truth. We must speak in a professional, loving, and confident voice that conveys our thoughts while making others comfortable. Speaking your mind gives you an opportunity to speak your heart. Trust yourself to speak kindly to others, to speak truthfully, to speak lovingly.

Trust in Others

When it was time for me to find someone to help care for my child, I felt as though I would never be able to trust anyone with such a significant job. I'm sure all mothers feel this way, but I was surprised at my inability to trust others. I knew I had to release the situation to God's hands. Then I started asking everyone and anyone whom they had found to care for their children. My heart broke whenever someone said "my mother" or "my aunt." I was living far from family members who could assist me. How could I find someone who would equal a grandmother or an aunt? Could I ever trust someone enough?

After visiting and interviewing more than 15 different women, I met a lady named Lovey. Her home was warm and inviting, clean and organized, and ideal for children. Her references used words such as: hardworking, honest, dependable, caring, nurturing, and trustworthy. My mind was now at ease. I was so happy I found someone I could trust to care for my little bundle of joy.

Through my experience with Lovey and many others I discovered I could not make it through life without trusting people. It was a lesson I embraced fully in the workplace. After all, I hired countless people and trusted them to work hard for my business. I learned to look for the characteristics that people of integrity demonstrate. We must learn very quickly how to identify the type of people we can trust if we want to live a full and successful life.

Develop Relationships for Growth

We will only grow in a positive direction if we plan our growth. Building key relationships is important to becoming successful. It is imperative to determine whom you are spending time with on a regular basis. Are these relationships stretching and pressing you toward your goals? A trap that is easy to fall into is to become the person in the group everyone looks to for advice. While they are growing from your knowledge, you will only grow as far as your capacity will take you.

I suggest you make a list of the areas you want to target for growth. Begin to search for people who can assist you in these areas. (Look back at your human resources list.) Call them and share what you are trying to accomplish. Invite them to lunch. Remember…when you invite you pay. Make an investment in yourself. You will be surprised how receptive people are to meet with you when a clear objective for the meeting is communicated.

Take the time to build productive relationships and watch your growth curve move forward full steam ahead.

Trust of Others

Earning the trust of others is based upon deserving their trust. Deserved trust is usually developed by displaying consistent behavior over time. Others watch to see if our actions match our word. We have all probably witnessed a conversation where one associate showers another with compliments and encouragement and then five minutes later turns to us in private and verbally tears down that same person. Unfortunately, I have experienced this many times. Such people are two-faced and choose to play a role to get what they want. I often wonder what they are saying about me when I walk away.

The above is the "don't" version of how to win friends and influence people. You must have and display integrity at all times. They must see that you walk your talk. Your compliments and comments should never be followed by sideways glances and insincere commentary. Live out your faith by bestowing grace and compassion on others. Not only will they trust you, they will discover what is in your heart.

Trust Between You and God

It is clear that God loves us and wants to trust us. He paid the ultimate price when He gave His Son to die for us. Now we have an opportunity to show God how much we love Him. We do this by living the life He has called us to live.

> Let love be without hypocrisy. Abhor what is evil. Cling
> to what is good. Be kindly affectionate to one another
> with brotherly love, in honor giving preference to one

another; not lagging in diligence, fervent in spirit, serving the Lord; rejoicing in hope, patient in tribulation, continuing steadfastly in prayer; distributing to the needs of the saints, given to hospitality. Bless those who persecute you; bless and do not curse. Rejoice with those who rejoice, and weep with those who weep. Be of the same mind toward one another. Do not set your mind on high things, but associate with the humble. Do not be wise in your own opinion. Repay no one evil for evil. Have regard for good things in the sight of all men. If it is possible, as much as depends on you, live peaceably with all men. Beloved, do not avenge yourselves, but rather give place to wrath; for it is written, "Vengeance is Mine, I will repay," says the Lord. Therefore "If your enemy is hungry, feed him; if he is thirsty, give him a drink; for in so doing you will heap coals of fire on his head." Do not be overcome by evil, but overcome evil with good (Romans 12:9-21).

Whew! Nobody said being a Christian was easy, but it is fulfilling. Trust God to lead you to your intended work and purpose. If we pray on the Romans verses today, and tomorrow we are insulted, attacked, or let down by another, we can respond the right way and keep the incident in perspective. We must learn to love those who persecute us and let God do the rest.

God wants to trust us in all aspects of our lives. In today's life much of our thoughts, actions, and decisions are based on finances…or lack thereof. When it comes to money and belongings, it is not just a matter of trust, but God *entrusting* us with such resources. Everything we have from Him is placed under our care. If money or blessings are misused rather than sown to bless others and God, we must take responsibility. Sadly, money can come to rule our life in place of faith. Do you think God will honor that kind of life? What kind of steward will you be if your priorities are all messed up?

In Matthew 25:15-30, Jesus walks us through the parable of the talents, which is a story about how to honor or dishonor the resources we are given. The short version: A landlord gave five talents to servant A, two talents to servant B, and one talent to servant C. Servant A traded with his five talents and made another five. Servant B took his two and gained two more. Servant C was afraid he would be reprimanded if he lost his one talent, so he dug a hole in the ground and hid the money. Much later the landlord returned to check on the resource management skills of his staff. To servants A and B he said, "Well done, good and faithful servant; you were faithful over a few things, I will make you ruler over many things. Enter into the joy of your lord."

But servant C received a talking to. "You wicked and lazy servant, you knew that I reap where I have not sown, and gather where I have not scattered seed. So you ought to have deposited my money with the bankers, and at my coming I would have received back my own with interest. Therefore take the talent from him, and give it to him who has ten talents. For to everyone who has, more will be given, and he will have abundance; but from him who does not have, even what he has will be taken away."

Jesus illustrates how He will bless us with more if we properly manage what we are already given. If we mismanage what comes from the Father's hand, why would He give us more to bury, squander, or ignore? God is the Creator and Manager of the universe—He wants to know if He can trust us with our time, resources, money, families, careers, companies, ministries, and blessings. Be sure you don't mistake items of affluence for blessings of significance. We shouldn't admire our shiny new car and pat ourselves on the back. For one thing, that car's earthly owner is probably the nearest savings and loan. Secondly, its heavenly owner is the Provider who is probably shaking His head at our driveway happy-dance and saying, "Child, that toy on wheels only serves the purpose of transportation. Don't turn it into a destination."

Don't we want everything God has for us? I lift my hands in praise for all that God has entrusted to me over the years. It took time because I needed to grow and mature in my faith to make room for what came next. Show Him you are able to handle little things well so He can release big things into your hands. Because we have been talking money, you are probably thinking ahead to the blessing of winning the lottery or receiving an unexpected inheritance. God doesn't work that way. If He did, Christianity would be about controlling God rather than having faith *in* God. Serve your Lord well. Empty your life of trappings and false idols. *Then* you will be able to receive the riches God has for you. A career change might be the blessing. A child. A trial that refines you. You see, blessings come in all kinds of packages. Can God trust you right now with a blessing?

Once we begin to trust ourselves, trust in others, earn the trust of others, and develop trust between ourselves and God, we will begin to see balance come into our life. Things will begin to click and success will be just around the corner. If you make a mistake along the way (and you will), question marks can fill the air between you and another person. Integrity can either be lost or it can be strengthened. It all depends on how you respond.

Rebuild Integrity

It is a very difficult position to be in when your actions or words call your integrity into question. Once you give someone reason to doubt, your every move and motive will fall under scrutiny and suspicion. Integrity is lost when there has been some type of breach in the relationship. Whether this happens on the job or with family or friends, it is vital to deal with this serious situation immediately. You might bank on the "time heals all wounds" theory, but the truth is that the more time that passes, the stronger the wound becomes. I have learned through experience that the only way to turn the situation around is to face it head-on as quickly as possible. The first step must be contacting the individual and apologizing. Explain what happened and why you chose the course of action in question.

Even if your decision was right or seemed right, acknowledge their feelings about the decision. It doesn't cost you anything to apologize, but it may cost you everything if you do not. By taking this step, you can avoid apologizing for the situation again and again through indirect ways…showing that person favoritism to make up for it, acting sheepish or timid in their presence, downplaying future successes out of guilt. These tactics will not serve you on your path to success, and they will not resolve the initial situation.

After you have apologized, show the person you are a person of integrity every day by displaying the characteristics of integrity. It might feel as though you are on probation, and in a way, you are. It might not feel fair, but the effort is necessary. That is what integrity is all about…making the effort and taking responsibility even if you are not asked to, even if your peers or coworkers do not uphold the same values that you do. Over time you will rebuild areas of broken trust, and those who were affected will no longer be watching for you to fail. They will be watching to see how a person of integrity moves on.

Principle Prayer

Lord of my life, thank You for all that You have entrusted to my hands and my heart. I pray to be considered worthy and righteous in Your sight. Lead my steps along the path of integrity. When I lose my footing and cause someone to question my integrity, give me courage to do what is best. May the way I talk, listen, lead, and follow model a life of integrity. Amen.

*P*rinciple in Practice

1. List the characteristics of a person of integrity. Are you lacking in any of these?

2. Start your own inspiration wall. Or use your journal or notebook to list people who uphold particular characteristics of integrity. Who inspires you?

3. How are you not loving and trusting yourself? Others?

4. List everything you can think of that God has given you. Evaluate if you are a good steward of those things in your life. Take steps to change, if you need to.

5. Do you have relationships you need to rebuild for the sake of integrity?

6. What relationships do you need for personal and professional growth?

7. What should you do to develop these friendships and relationships?

Step into Leadership

Take action on your vision with a servant's heart.
Be willing to accept the responsibilities, accolades,
and adversities of leadership with a gracious spirit.

"Well done, good and faithful servant; you were
faithful over a few things, I will make you ruler
over many things. Enter into the joy of your
lord."

MATTHEW 25:21

A bird's-eye view of me getting ready for work must be com-
ical. I zip back and forth from my closet to my desk gathering what
I need in order to be clothed and prepared for the day. On this
particular morning, my television was turned on and my favorite
Christian station served as background inspiration. I struggled
to get my earrings in place while selecting a pair of shoes when
my mind started to pick up on the message being shared by Pastor
Paula White. She was teaching a powerful word on the goodness
of God and all He has for us. At first I only caught bits and pieces,
and then I realized this was not just *her* message, but also God's
message for me that day. I sat down on the edge of my bed and
took it all in with an open heart. The personal agenda I had that
morning was replaced by God's plan for me.

God, please let me be receptive to what You have to share with me. My prayer opened my heart to fully absorb the words Paula spoke. It was as if I were the only one she was speaking to. I know her message touched many lives, but it sure seemed she got up this morning with me in mind. No, she didn't know me. That didn't matter. She and I knew the same mighty God, and He was doing a good work in my life that morning.

After she finished preaching, Pastor White mentioned her boot camp that was taking place in Lakeland, Florida, in a couple of weeks. Pow! God began to speak to me. It was time to shift my life toward the ministry He told me about eight years ago in my hospital room. The season was now, and this conference was the next step. He would use this event to reveal details about my new vision and future. I allowed myself to question this for only a moment. *Maybe hardworking Victoria is just trying to find a way to take a vacation during a stressful time?* But I am a resourceful person, and I could think of plenty of places I could go for a vacation other than Lakeland, Florida—a place I had never heard of…to listen to a woman I was barely familiar with…to get God's directions for my life. Only He would create such a scenario and convince me to follow. As I wrote down the website and telephone information, God assured my heart and spirit with, "Victoria, even though you do not know exactly why I am sending you to this conference, you must go by faith and trust Me to be true to My word."

I informed my assistant, Carla, that I needed to get to Lakeland, Florida, because I was going to Pastor Paula White's conference. Her look of confusion was followed by a rush of logical questions. "Where is that? Who is that? And why would you interrupt your current busy schedule for this?" My response didn't really appease her, but it was all I could offer. "I do not know where Lakeland,

Florida, is. I cannot tell you much about Pastor White, but I need to attend this event because I am following God's lead. He is going to teach me something…something I need to learn right now."

Next, I called my sister, who had a broken ankle at the time, and asked her to attend the conference. I don't know if it was the thrill of getting away from home or my promise that this event would be important to my vision, but my sweet, willing sister agreed. By the time the day of the trip arrived, I was filled with great anticipation and wonder. I just couldn't imagine what God had in store for me. Along the way, He made an interesting promise to my heart. "I will usher you in." Usher me in? I had visions of God motioning me to my seat like an opera-house usher. This image made me laugh. So the all-powerful God is now working at weekend conferences in Lakeland, Florida? This I *had* to see.

By the way, Lakeland is physically between Tampa and Orlando, Florida. But spiritually, Lakeland was between my now and my future.

Leaders Follow Directions

It is nothing short of a miracle what God will do *with* and *through* our lives when we allow Him to take full control. A great leader must not only learn to follow, they must know whom to follow. To experience lasting success, we must have only one leader—God. By following God, we become His servant. You might abide by a system of authority in the workplace and the country's government, but the leader of your mind, body, spirit, and life should be God alone. We must be willing to perform the deeds He created us to do. "For we are His workmanship, created in Christ Jesus for good works, which God prepared beforehand that we should walk in them" (Ephesians 2:10).

The key to receiving your orders from the Creator is to develop a relationship with Him. This allows us to clearly hear what He wants us to do and where He wants us to lead. We will go nowhere if someone gives us explicit directions and we are not listening to the information. The lines of communication between our hearts and God are only open when we have an intimate relationship with Him.

As you have figured out by now, I hear from God in a way that feels very direct and personal. One of my girlfriends is always asking me about this. "How can you hear God? How is that possible?" When we meet for lunch and I am filled from a time of prayer and conversation with the Lord, she looks at me and shakes her head. Now, this friend *does* hear God...just in a different manner. She loves the Lord, and He guides her in a way she will heed. For my life, God speaks in a whisper to my heart. For others, God probably does a little shoutin' from time to time. I think maybe God whispers to me because this is how He caught my attention when I was in the hospital praying for my unborn baby. Gentle nudging might have gone unnoticed in the rush of hospital procedures, doctor's instructions, and the beating of my heart. And a shout might have sent me into a panic. God whispered because He knew I would hear Him loud and clear.

Meanwhile, Somewhere in Florida...

When we arrived at the auditorium in Lakeland, I could not believe how many people were standing in line. Our late showing placed us toward the back of a long line of probably 3000 folks. My sister limped along, and I knew her willing spirit would give way to regret if I didn't figure out a plan. "You go on inside," I said. "Sit in the foyer, and then when I get close to the front, I will call you on your cell phone." As much as I wanted her company,

I knew this was best. And she needed no convincing. So off she went and I reshuffled my stance a few times and waited.

But not for long.

Though I had laughed at the image of God working as an usher, my mouth was too wide open in surprise to laugh when a woman approached me and told me, "You are supposed to be inside." What? I told her she must have me confused with someone else. No. She insisted that I was supposed to be brought inside and led to a special seating section. Now, if my sister had been with me, I would have assumed this surprise kindness was the act of someone taking pity on the woman with a broken ankle. But I stood there alone at the back of the line. This is what it looks like when God keeps His promise—it is the most ordinary and the most extraordinary moment you can imagine.

A faithful leader knows when to release her hold on the world and the world's ways. I could have spent the rest of the conference trying to figure out how my sister and I ended up with great seats, but then I would have missed out on being a good servant. Because every godly leader understands she is just a servant using her natural gifts while waiting to be ushered into God's purpose and presence.

Committed to the Vision

A successful leader is totally committed to bringing her vision to life. God might bring the vision to you at what seems to be an awkward time, or when you feel least prepared, but leadership involves risk and steps of faith. Or in some cases…leaps.

A clearer look at my vision unfolded during the conference. My ministry would serve to inspire and motivate women and men to fulfill their purpose and build up godly businesses, new ventures, and dreams. The biggest surprise was…He meant now…right away. *Get ready, set, go, Victoria.* For some reason I was shocked. *He wants me to start the ministry now? Is it a good time to start? Am I ready to begin a ministry? How will I support the ministry financially? What will others think?* The questions were coming so fast I barely kept up with my own thoughts.

But why was I shocked? God told me more than eight years ago that He was going to turn my business success into an open door for ministry. This situation made me think about Jesus coming back. I am certain He's returning someday, but am I really ready? I was certain I would be in the ministry someday, but was I ready for it to be now? To be surprised by God is an amazing experience. You stand in awe because you know there is nothing more powerful, more loving, more all-knowing than your Creator. I saw myself and my life in the palm of His hand. I was excited, but I also understood just how serious and important this day was in my life.

Because I am committed to my vision, I will do whatever God sends me to do. The answers to the questions I was asking were irrelevant. They were about me holding on to the world and holding on to the limitations and worries of Victoria Lowe. Becoming the best leader I could be meant I had to release my grip and reach for God's hand.

Take Action

I am concerned that many of us will never experience living our dreams because we are not willing to do what is required to make this happen. While I risk sounding negative, I am deeply troubled by what I see going on around me. There is a lot of talk action about living our purpose, vision, and dreams. But not many people are actually putting the *process of achievement* into action. We have become comfortable just reading and talking about dreams. During the past few years, I have discovered just how difficult it is to put down the book on dreams and hang up the phone while talking about my dreams so I can pick up my vision statement and begin to take the first steps.

My comments are not meant to deter you. My goal is to inspire you to step out by faith and take that first step. I realize now, today, this moment may seem like the wrong time. We can talk about the economy not being right, our personal obligations being too heavy, our commitments being too set in stone, but if we do that, there will never be a perfect time. And, my friend, you will never get this moment back, so make good use of it by getting started.

Let's start by turning over our entire lives to God. Give Him full control of everything. We must allow Him to manage our:

- time
- resources
- money
- family/friends
- health
- careers
- businesses

Are you ready? Let's turn it all over to Him. If I could, I would sit beside you and help pry your fingers from all the burdens and responsibilities you hold on to so tightly. There is no looking back now; it's full steam ahead. A great leader must be willing to let go. This should be the first lesson taught in leadership training. Unfortunately, most of what we are taught and shown indicates the opposite. Many people in society equate leadership with acquiring, taking over, buying out, and expanding. Teachers and those discussing leadership leave out that significant first step of letting go. Don't be swayed by the world's viewpoint. When you give control over to God from the very start, you are well on your way.

Great Leaders Build Great Teams

A leader is not a leader unless someone is following. You might write off that statement as not being very profound, but it is a concept that not all leaders understand. When one is given authority or has earned a position of control, there is a tendency to alienate others for the sake of self-preservation. Successful leaders recognize that everyone under their authority is part of a team. Whether they are family members, friends, employees, vendors, customers, or members, they are all teammates. And when you step into the lead, one of your primary responsibilities is to determine the role they will each play on the team.

In the NBA, the managers and coaches must choose a team of people representing diverse skills and abilities. If everyone shoots and nobody blocks or plays defense, they end up a pretty useless group out on the court. And can you imagine the arguments that would arise? Everyone would want to do what they are good at…shoot the ball. That game would go nowhere fast. But the team that has a diverse selection of skills—and honors those skills—will be the successful team.

Manage and Nurture Relationships

A great leader must manage teammate relationships. At best, we manage our relationships with our companies, employees, and clients, but we tend to misunderstand how important it is to manage our relationships with family and friends. All of our relationships will provide support for our vision if we include them in the process. In your personal relationships, lead by example. In your professional relationships, provide your team members with skill development, training, and open communication policies that foster unity, security, and support.

A strong leader is able to recognize when to lead the team and when to let the team lead themselves. Some people in authority don't necessarily realize this is good leadership. From their limited viewpoint, they didn't sweat through ten years of hard work just to step aside and give a team space to maneuver. But they should. I have learned over the years that if I do not allow the team to perform on its own in certain circumstances, the members grow too dependent on my leadership alone. I might go home at the end of the day having satisfied my need for control, but this false security would eventually be replaced by exhaustion and ineffectiveness. I would end up with a team of people incapable of success.

Raising a child presents the same dilemma. If a parent runs around picking out clothes, running bath water, making lunches, and taking over homework assignments, the child does not learn. I admit that I have to resist doing too much for my daughter. I want to be helpful or I want to be sure a task is done correctly. Either way, I am not helping Briana become successful. I am hindering her development, and I am hurting my family, my personal support team. This is not strong parenting, nor is it strong leadership.

Attitude Check, Please

If we for one instant view leadership as the responsibility to keep others down or in one place, I guarantee that our company, church, or community will not reach the goals it could or should. Either we are for growth or against it…and I don't just mean our own.

The simple choice to give others room to blossom in their purpose will turn an average team into a mighty one. The only way to learn how to lead is to practice leading. You did it at some point; now let your team have the same opportunity. They will struggle with leading the first couple of times, but eventually the skills will become second nature.

Learn to Listen

"Come on over sometime, Victoria. I would like you to watch my leadership in action."

Let's say you extended this invitation to me, and I said, "Sure thing," grabbed a notebook, an audio recorder, and showed up the next day unannounced. I sat quietly in the corner of your office, conference room, or living room for a day and recorded all of the conversations that took place. Would you hear what I hear? An outsider can often more clearly discern what is being said and how it is being communicated than someone who is faced with the same people, decisions, and styles of dialogue every day.

Listening is a requirement of leadership. Since you invited me to drop in on you, I will share with you what I have found. I invite you to lunch, pull out the recorder, press play, and ask you to listen, really listen, to your leadership. Think about the following questions and your situation:

- Would I hear actual dialogue or would I hear you presenting monologues?
- Would I hear that the cochair of your committee is not clear about your vision?

- Would I detect your unwillingness to let your team lead by the way you negate their suggestions and build up your own?

- Would I hear you asking for specific results or vague objectives?

Many leaders make the mistake of doing most of the talking. It is very difficult to stay in tune with what is going on when you are doing all the yadda yadda-ing. Someone once said, "We are supposed to listen twice as much as we talk, that's why God gave us two ears and one mouth." Put those two ears to good use.

Teach to Win

People must be taught how to win over and over again because winning does not always look the same. In one case it is landing a big contract, and in another it is pulling together as a team to complete a demanding project. Winning is not always a situation involving competition with another person, company, or team. Winning is just as significant when it involves achieving our personal best.

Give your team a vision of what winning will look like in each situation. Provide them with the tools they need so they will use them automatically. And when the finish line is crossed and the accolades are handed out, a winning leader shares the spotlight with the entire team. It is not acceptable for the leader to be the only one out front. If this were acceptable, then it would be just as acceptable for your team members to leave every aspect of the next project on your plate. The "doing" is as important as the "achieving and receiving" stage of a big win or big effort.

Now and then you do lose. We don't have to like it, but it is part of learning and part of success. When you must bear a loss, a victorious spirit of excellence should still be evident. You can identify the faulty areas of your original plan. You can start to fix those problems and train up others to do the same. But before you do any of that, show your integrity by acknowledging the loss, recognizing where things went well, and appreciating those who gave their best along the way. Part of becoming a great leader is learning how to win with humility and lose with dignity. If you model this for your teammates, you will replace the human urge to blame and shame with the godly desire to claim the victory waiting just around the corner.

The Cost of Leadership

I have had conversations with men and women who are flying high on their rising star yet confused about why they are still plagued with worries. Successful leadership replaces one set of problems with another. But the good news for a successful, faithful leader is that once you can recognize the concerns, you are already equipped with the skills and the wisdom to handle them.

Everyone Is Watching

One high cost of leadership is accepting or handling public scrutiny when you make a decision. And there is always someone who will disagree with your decision. I have found public opinion to be friend and foe. People will keep everything moving forward, and they can be your biggest fans and support system. But when they are disgruntled, they can make life stressful. When I think of this cost of leadership, I think of a pastor's life. I don't know how pastors deal with public scrutiny. (Well, I do…they rely on God's grace and strength.) Almost everything pastors do or say seems to be public knowledge and under committee approval.

Pastors may be told this goes along with the territory, but it cannot be easy. Standing on the front line and having the entire congregation critique your work and decisions requires excellent leadership skills and a lot of patience.

Even with scrutiny at every turn, a leader must hold steadfast to the decisions she has made. A leader cannot be viewed as wishy-washy. We must spend time researching and analyzing our decisions, because once we take a stand it is difficult for others and for our vision if we change our position. However, if a mistake has been made or a change in circumstances has arisen, a leader must accept the burden of redirecting the team. Just be clear what your alternative route will be before you start replacing everyone's priorities. When you are ready to communicate the changes, be empathetic about how the change will impact the team members. Their perspectives should be heard. Listen. Then lead on in the new direction you have outlined. Reveal the new strategy with enthusiasm, confidence, and sensitivity. Your team will be taking their cues from you.

Tough Calls Are Yours to Make

Tough decisions can consume you. They will rise up like giant walls to block your path. But a successful leader surveys that wall, has topographical maps drawn, and plans the solution to overcome this barrier. When a tough decision comes into play, this is not the time to test the leadership skills of the team. A leader must use her position and experience to protect the team and model good decision making. When I have any decision to make, I turn to my partner in life...God. He finds me on my knees praying frequently and in the strangest places.

Many times tough calls require the leader to take calculated risks. There may or may not be a proven solution. During these times a leader must assess that risk, pray for guidance, and listen to God's leading. Because leadership is an act of faith rather than a proven science, you have to roll with the punches. And there will be punches.

Transition and Change

Over the course of my 17 years in business, one of the toughest lessons I have had to learn is to make changes quickly and adapt to change instantaneously. The best leaders are those who realize a situation or environment has changed and make the appropriate adjustments right away. This may require a leader to make very difficult decisions, such as: walking away from one of your most valuable clients, closing branches, laying off some of your favorite employees, or writing off invoices for a client.

While leadership is very complex and comprehensive, it is vital to have strong leadership skills if we want to win and be successful in life. Whether you are a stay-at-home mom, secretary, nurse, novelist, corporate team member, or the CEO of a 20-million-dollar company, sharp leadership skills allow you to manage the responsibilities that come with the role or position in which God has placed you.

Called to Change

The vision that has carried you for fifteen years or five or one might be changed by God's direction and movement in your life; you must be prepared to accept that. The leadership training and experience gained in one setting might be the platform God intended for a new thing. The good work God is doing can take you many directions.

My transition into ministry required and continues to require stepping outside of my comfort zone. God knows we are more likely to reach for His hand when we are entering vulnerable, unknown territory. We seek His protection, His direction, His power. I had become very comfortable walking as a leader in the business arena. I had memorized all the game rules. I knew the faces and personalities of the team players...and they knew me. Now God has me walking in a totally new arena. I am trying to absorb the new rules of conduct; I am adapting my view of leadership for this expansion of my vision. The application of these spiritual principles provides me with a plan I can trust, even when the route seems bumpy.

When you are committed to the vision God gives you, you must be willing to step up and out. In many cases you will be asked to do things and go places you do not understand, especially if you are allowing God to lead the way. Some of the tasks may make other people around you feel as though you are losing touch with reality. When I packed up and headed to Lakeland, Florida, I know a few people on my corporate team thought (and may still believe) I was losing it. They were shaking their heads the way my mother did eight years ago, saying "What in the world? Where is the rational, grounded Victoria we know?" But the difference between their perspective and mine is that I see the future plan for today's actions. I know I am following a vision for my life. And I had to be ready to accept God's call to push forth in the new direction— the direction I knew would be mine to follow when my Lord said "now is the time."

A leader must be willing to step out and do whatever she can to further the vision she has been given. Trust the Lord. He is preparing you to become a leader in the quest for your own vision.

Principle Prayer

Creator and Leader of my life, I praise You for the opportunities I have to serve You by leading others. May I always pay attention to the needs of my team. Guide my words to offer encouragement and inspiration to those who work with me. Remind me to lead by example and to let others lead when it is their time. I know that my efforts as a leader should build up the kingdom. Lead me on in Your purpose, Lord. I will follow. Amen.

*P*rinciple in Practice

1. Determine whether you are following God or something/someone else.

2. Listen for God's direction before you make another decision.

3. Assess the skills and abilities of your team. How can you help them grow, learn to lead, and serve the vision at hand?

4. Practice listening this week. Tune in not only to words, but to body language and behaviors as well. Write down in your journal what you have learned.

5. Is change in the air for you? Are you trying to hold on to any directions or circumstances God is asking you to change? Pray about these.

PART THREE:
Blessing

*G*ive Along the Way

Give of yourself and your resources to God's success for you.

> "But this I say: He who sows sparingly will also
> reap sparingly, and he who sows bountifully will
> also reap bountifully. So let each one give as he
> purposes in his heart, not grudgingly or of neces-
> sity; for God loves a cheerful giver. And God is
> able to make all grace abound toward you, that
> you, always having all sufficiency in all things,
> may have abundance for every good work."
>
> 2 CORINTHIANS 9:6-8

Real success is achieved when we are able to extend our hand to the community and world that God uses to bless us. Success is defined by our ability to bless others.

The Look of Success

Unfortunately, many see success as a great storehouse of material belongings. We picture a big house, luxury cars, designer clothes, and first-class travel. If you are caught up in this definition or surround yourself with others who live by this definition, it is time to assess your success. "For everything in the world— the cravings of sinful man, the lust of his eyes and the boasting of what he has and does—comes not from the Father but from the world. The world and its desires pass away, but the man who does the will of God lives forever" (1 John 2:16-17 NIV). Icons of status and beauty do not go on to great things; these worldly desires *pass away.* And if our sense of value and worth are attached, they will deteriorate right along with them.

Okay, get your "stinking thinking" out in the open here. "But people love me when I have such things. They notice me and seem pleased with me." Friend, that kind of affection is designer-clothing deep. "Command those who are rich in this present age not to be haughty, nor trust in uncertain riches, but in the living God, who gives us richly all things to enjoy" (1 Timothy 6:17). Admiration and love from others is not heartfelt unless they have seen and felt the riches of your heart and spirit. So assess your view of success. If *giving* does not carry the weight of *receiving* in your definition, you will never achieve true success.

Empty Achievement

Several years ago I visited an old friend who had become very accomplished in the business world. I was a little uncomfortable staying with her because it had been so long since we had seen one another, and I didn't want to impose. Perhaps I harbored those sneaky insecurities that arise when we face high school reunions and other "long time, no see" events. But my friend graciously insisted that I stay with her, and my worry turned into the anticipation of catching up, sharing memories, and meeting her family.

As I stepped into the grand foyer of her house, my eyes took in amazing fabrics, rich wood trim, floor-to-ceiling windows, pristine furniture, and exotic accent pieces. Beautiful possessions and collections were on display everywhere. I was very happy and proud to see all the comforts my friend's success had provided, but while taking a tour of this personal palace, I felt the chill of emptiness and loneliness. The warm and cozy feeling that resides in a house filled with love was absent. You know the kind—the home where the aroma of good food encircles the laughter and conversation of family and friends. The kind of space where people gather to share stories and lives. But in this beautiful house, the only aroma was the citrus scent of furniture polish. And the rooms were hollow, austere, and longing for laughter.

My first impression was reinforced that night at dinner. Family members who had been in their respective rooms to watch television or work on projects came to the kitchen only long enough to eat a quick meal or prepare a plate and return to their rooms. When the family did speak to one another, the dialogue consisted of requests or necessary information. Emptiness rattled around in that house and proclaimed the truth that this family was not happy and had not achieved real success. They had lost one another on their way to the perfect life.

By the last day of my stay, I ached for my friend. In the awkward silence of that home, I felt led to ask her if she was okay. My heart broke when I realized she had not been asked that in a very long time. The floodgates opened. She shared with me how miserable they had become. The work of obtaining and maintaining material success had taken over the work of maintaining emotional success. Personal goals replaced team efforts. Material possessions filled rooms where love once thrived.

I was changed by that visit. It was as if I had been walking around with blinders on and God ripped them off the moment I returned to my own home. I realized, much to my surprise, that

I was headed toward a similar sickness. While my family and I still communicated, the signs of the same syndrome echoed through the house. The rooms were not warm and cozy. Most of our meals were eaten separately. We had all the trimmings of success, but real success did not live in our home either. It was as if I had spent time with Dickens' ghost of the future and was being given a chance to change. I no longer wanted to wake up each day with the goal of just surviving. I wanted to greet each new beginning with a smile on my face and love and passion in my heart. I wanted our home to be a place where family and friends could give and receive the simple joys of love and community.

The Greatest Gift

The basis of all true gifts is love. "This is My commandment, that you love one another as I have loved you" (John 15:12). We can read this commandment followed by a heartfelt "Amen!" but what does loving one another look like? We can list the lessons we teach our children so they will get along with others at school: play nicely, help others, share kind words, and so on. But our call, our command to love one another, goes deeper than this. We must be willing to give ourselves. Personally, I think it is easier to give our money than it is to give our selves. Write a check and you are done. But if someone needs time or a commitment from us, that positive response turns into "Um, let me look at my schedule and get back to you." Right? Our effort to create an orderly world feels disrupted when we have to extend ourselves.

Well, God does not call us to be cheerleaders who just "rah-rah" at those who need help. He asks us to get in the game. To actively love one another. And godly giving may involve some tough work on our part. We are asked to put aside the hurts of our past. Most of us have been hurt by people we loved, so to trust and give a part of ourselves without a guarantee can feel risky. Yet isn't it interesting that one of the most difficult things to give comes with the most rewards?

"Now abide faith, hope, love, these three; but the greatest of these is love" (1 Corinthians 13:13). Love is the greatest and most powerful emotion. It is so powerful that poets, scientists, pastors, and philosophers spend a good portion of their lives trying to define it. Ask 20 people on the street for a description of love, and you will probably receive 20 different answers. But while we may not be able to define love, we know when we feel it. When we are *in love*, we feel warm, satisfied, and complete. When we love someone, we also want what is best for them. We take it upon ourselves to become a part of what it takes to make them happy. This is when love is put in motion.

Love can also be very painful. When we see someone we care for participating in harmful activities, it becomes very difficult to watch. Our protective nature wants to keep them from harm or sickness. Our love can be so strong that when they hurt, we physically hurt as well. When I visit loved ones who are ill, something inside of me feels ill. Many times there is nothing we can do but pray for them. In the corridor of the hospital, at their bedside, in a treatment center waiting room, we feel helpless. Yet relying on God is a way to love the one in pain or the one we are unable to protect.

Sharing God's Love

Our communion with God and our pursuit of His Word leads us to love as He intended. In 1 Corinthians 13:1-8, we receive a clear picture of the type of love God wants us to have for one another. The essence of this love is laid out within the 16 characteristics listed below:

1. Love suffers long—has patience with imperfect people

2. Love is kind—is attentive and compassionate

3. Love does not envy—is never possessive and is noncompetitive

4. Love does not parade itself—does not show off

5. Love is not puffed up—is never filled with arrogance and pride

6. Love does not behave rudely—displays good manners and courtesy

7. Love does not seek its own—is unselfish and giving

8. Love is not provoked—is gracious

9. Love thinks no evil—does not keep account of wrong doings

10. Love does not rejoice in iniquity—will not celebrate the shortcomings of others

11. Love rejoices in truth—advertises and celebrates goodness and God

12. Love bears all things—defends and holds up

13. Love believes—believes the best of others

14. Love hopes all things—will not give up on people

15. Love endures all things—preserves and is loyal to the end

16. Love never fails—never quits, gives up, or betrays

Love is selfless, giving, and endures forever. I have included the 16 characteristics of love because they offer us a model, a glimpse of what love looks like. As Christians, we are blessed to see love in the person of Jesus Christ. We experience it in His grace and forgiveness. We pass it on to others out of thankfulness.

Natural Givers

On Saturday afternoons I sometimes enjoy sitting at the mall or park observing people. I love to watch teenagers make their rounds from store to store in a giggling group. I see older couples walk hand in hand alongside the lake. This personal pastime helps me appreciate that people are natural givers. Some might write off teenagers as self-absorbed or immature, but I have witnessed them returning someone's lost bag. I have seen them put their arms around a friend who is downcast. And my heart leaps at the sight of an elderly husband reaching for the hand of his love to help her across the bridge. Leviticus 19:18 says, "You shall love your neighbor as yourself." God planned from the beginning that we would take care of one another. The natural giver was a part of God's original plan.

Giving Is Better Than Receiving

Once we achieve real success, we will enjoy giving more than receiving. This is a cliché, but I firmly believe that it is better to give than to receive. The privilege of giving is a gift itself. Have you ever selected the perfect present for a friend and watched as the person opened it with delight? Have you ever provided a needed resource to a family and seen how it changed their lives? It makes the heart beat with new joy. We understand how the spirit opens up and grows large and strong through acts of sacrifice, giving, and kindness.

We have all seen the bumper sticker that reads: "Commit random acts of kindness." I say, let's commit random *and* planned acts of kindness. Make it a deliberate part of your daily mission and life vision to give as a reflection of the Giver.

As writer Henri Nouwen observed, the act of giving is transformed when it is a response to grace. "When gratitude is the source of our actions, our giving becomes receiving and those to whom we minister become our ministers."[1] The Lord provides for the spiritual well-being of His children when they give in His name. "Each one should use whatever gift he has received to serve others, faithfully administering God's grace in its various forms" (1 Peter 4:10 NIV). God does not bless us for ourselves. He blesses us so we can bless and serve someone else. He gives to us so we can give to someone else. He leads us so we can lead someone else. He offers us grace so we can offer grace to someone else.

Giving Our Resources

If we are blessed with financial success and security, we might find that receiving more is nice but does not hold the same thrill it used to. I have a confession...I love shoes. When I started to earn money, I would reward myself by going out and buying a new pair. Now, years later, I still enjoy checking out the latest styles, but my real thrill is stumbling across something that is perfect for one of my family members or friends. Even if I've had a particularly difficult day at work, my spirit lightens. God plants in our hearts the impulse to give. There is a little switch inside that turns on when we see someone in need or a need to fill. As we pursue our purpose, may we never rush by opportunities to meet the needs around us. The journey to real success includes many stops to help those people God brings to our attention.

How Much?

How to give and how much to give are sometimes points of confusion and even controversy. Over the years I have talked to many people about their feelings related to this topic. I have found that most people are not clear on what they personally should do; they are searching to understand the principle of giving. Christians primarily think of giving in terms of tithing, but they have many questions such as: Should I give everything to the church and let them provide for the community? Should I divide my giving between the church and the community? What does being a good steward look like? If we own a business, how should we give from that revenue?

People want to do the right thing. That is a great place to start as we seek answers. Below I will address the main concerns I hear most often and provide some insight and guidance to help you make your decisions.

How Much and How Often Should I Give?

This answer is very easy and structured. The Bible makes it clear in Malachi 3:10: "Bring all the tithes into the storehouse, that there may be food in My house." Typically, tithing means the practice of offering to God a tenth of our income. And income is the amount of gain received in a period of time. "When you receive from the Israelites the tithe I give you as your inheritance, you must present a tenth of that tithe as the LORD's offering. Your offering will be reckoned to you as grain from the threshing floor or juice from the winepress. In this way you also will present an offering to the LORD from all the tithes you receive from the Israelites" (Numbers 18:25-28 NIV). God tells us we are expected to offer Him a tenth of what we receive. Notice He says to bring the tithes *and* offerings into the storehouse. An offering is a presenting of something for acceptance. And God calls our offering to be above and beyond our tithe. It is a humble act of sacrifice and an expression of gratitude. And it is our own personal responsibility to decide what *offering* is acceptable to bring into the house of the Lord.

God expects us to bring Him our best when we make an offering. This is not about rounding up leftovers or gifts that require little sacrifice. The spirit of excellence...doing your very best...becomes the practice of giving your very best to the Lord.

When to give your tithes and offerings depends on your personal situation and preference. An easy way to stay on track is to give to the Lord as frequently as you receive your paycheck. I give God His share before I find a way to *spend* His share. Others may choose to do it differently, and as long as we offer the ten percent we owe Him it does not matter. Just don't get into the habit of writing God a mental IOU. I believe it is unacceptable to spend God's money and then try to replace it. True giving is not running up a spiritual tab.

Should I Give Based on My Gross or Net Income?

I have heard this question brought up since I was a kid. I think the best approach is to try to determine what God is saying through the following verse: "You shall truly tithe all the increase of your grain that the field produces year by year" (Deuteronomy 14:22). This tells us we are to give ten percent of every increase we take in. The gross amount of your paycheck might be $1000, but your actual increase is the $750 you see after taxes.

If you put $200 in your 401K, the $200 is still a part of your increase. To become very technical we should also tithe on the earnings we receive on our investments, because these too are increases. Giving beyond such increases is our opportunity to bless the house of the Lord with our offerings.

Whom Should We Give To?

Let's revisit Malachi 3:10. "Bring all the tithes into the storehouse, that there may be food in My house." God's house is the church. Our tithe provides financial backing for the church and its work. So what about those other worthy organizations, the homeless man you walk by on the way to the store each week, or the neighbor who is out of work? As Christians guided by the Holy Spirit, we see and sense needs at every turn. And of course, many of them are worthy causes, but God does not call you to all of them. Pray for discernment and then set aside a portion of your budget for these varied ways to give. Maybe you will commit to support a missionary or provide grocery money for a single mother. Follow that tug of your heart and then enter into this giving with a spirit of commitment and obedience. This is your offering.

Should I Give from My Business Income? If So, Should I Tithe off My Company's Income or My Salary?

If the increase or benefit we receive from the company is a salary, then we are required to tithe on the increase from that salary. If we take a dividend payout or any other type of payout from the company, then we need to tithe on this increase.

Business owners or partners are fortunate to have additional opportunities to make offerings to their Lord. Perhaps you provide programs that help increase the financial stability of your employees; your benefits package and the way you honor your staff can be viewed as an offering. Does your company participate in community efforts by giving donations, matching employee donations, or even allowing your employees to spend paid hours volunteering for important local agencies? You can really be creative when it is your company or a company in which you have influence. Listen to your staff and employees. What is on their hearts? What offerings can your business community make that fit your corporate mission and vision statement?

If we have a heart for God like David's, then giving offerings will be a natural part of our financial game plan. Psalm 20:3-4 says, "May He remember all your offerings, and accept your burnt sacrifice. May He grant you according to your heart's desire, and fulfill all your purpose." I believe God will honor the heart and purpose of your business when you model the principle of giving back to Him.

Different Gifts

Money is only one of the many ways to give to God and His children. I'd like you to open your mind and think beyond the donation coin box. God enriches our lives and we bless others when we give our time, knowledge, experiences, belongings, and most importantly ourselves.

Time

Here's an idea for a great gift. What if we went to the hospital one afternoon a month and spent time visiting people who never received visitors? Taking and making the time to enrich another person's life is time well spent. While such decisions do not interfere with our budgets, they do require sacrifice and commitment. Therefore, consider these decisions carefully and wisely, just as you would a financial commitment.

Resources, Knowledge, and Experiences

As a business owner, I carve out two hours a week to mentor other entrepreneurs. I make this time a priority by incorporating it into my weekly calendar. When I am rushed by other work-related obligations, I still reserve those times. During those times of sharing, I am blessed to pass along my knowledge and experience with others. My prayer is that mentoring will inspire others to grow and develop their own businesses. These meetings are very exciting for me. Fifteen minutes into the conversation I become passionate and intrigued by the same ideas that motivated me to pursue business in the first place. I am given a chance to help strategize the building of other companies, which allows me to leave a legacy in the business community.

Mentoring involves sharing the "lessons learned" in whatever your area of expertise might be. I bare my soul and confess the trials, struggles, and mistakes I have gone through because it gives the people I meet with a vision of how to handle down times as well as moments of success. I am able to share that God sustains me at all times. I give back to the Lord by giving Him the glory.

Whether you enjoy painting, reading, writing, or bird-watching, you have a chance to share your enthusiasm with someone else through mentoring. At your church you can share your spiritual experience and wisdom. Teach a class, disciple young girls, or mentor other women. I encourage you to return to the list of abilities and strengths you explored while discovering your purpose and vision. If you give from these areas of ability and joy, your offering will be pure and please the Lord.

Stuff

Don't we all have scary closets filled with items we no longer use? Or corners of our homes where we have boxes labeled "stuff to deal with later"? Well, I am all for purging possessions...and even more in favor of passing things along to folks who could make use of my belongings. I have found individuals or companies to take most of my household items. Furniture, clothing, books, new hygiene items, and bedding are of great use to shelters.

I suggest that you set aside a Saturday every two or three months to sift through your items. Make it a family activity: Order pizza, play fun music, and send your children off to their rooms or toy chests. Once they capture the joy and spirit of sharing, they will delight in these family days of giving. And a wonderful side benefit is that their rooms often become more orderly!

Me, Myself, and I

Look at your life as you would that hallway closet. What is it you are storing up rather than using? What gifts and abilities and resources remain on the shelves of your heart when they could serve the heart of your community, church, or organization? We must take an inventory of our physical, emotional, and spiritual selves. Ask God to show you how to share your true self. As is the case with all times of giving, this revelation will lead you to a deeper sense of who you are and help you stay on track with your vision and ultimate purpose. Nurture and share those parts of you that are in line with your calling. Your journey will be lighter and your steps more certain.

Learn to Give Up

Give up? How can giving up be a part of a plan for success?

Over the last few years, God has taught me that a big part of the principle of giving is understanding when and what to give up. I consider myself a fighter, so giving up seems too close to quitting for comfort. And I never like to quit or lose. When the battles come, my first response is to put on my armor and fight. But I have discovered that God does not intend for us to fight some battles. His intentions are for us to learn to give up and give in to His ways. Through the process of giving up, we are not losing the battle—we are only giving ourselves over to God's plan for our refinement and preparation for success in His will.

Giving up requires letting go of bad habits, false teachings, misconceptions, pride, and the desire for control. Oh my. There are some things I have held on to for dear life, and God was just patting me on the head and saying, "This is not yours to carry, dear. Why are you so stubborn?" If you have ever weaned a child from her pacifier or raggedy blanket, you know how God feels when He tries to take something from our grip. We are certain that nothing can replace the comfort and security of an ever-present mouthpiece or piece of material. Yet God is offering His comfort and security. Out of ignorance and fear we can end up playing tug-of-war over false idols.

Maybe we are holding tightly to a position God has called us to leave, or a priority that is not in His plan. Maybe one of our dreams has derailed our vision rather than moving us forward.

And a big one for many of us: We hold on to the past with a vengeance. We allow bad relationships, regrettable decisions, and open wounds from childhood to bind us to yesterday and keep us from fully experiencing tomorrow.

Faith for a Future

God wants to give us a future. A new beginning. A new work. Only when we will trust Him to take our raggedy burdens and barriers from our grasp will we discover the abundance of the new space He is creating for us. To believe this new space is a secure, solid place—and not the jagged cliff we imagine—requires us to have faith. This new direction requires us to surrender to His will so He can take us to the next level.

When my company first came out of bankruptcy, we were struggling financially. I had to turn everything over to God. The three-year battle took its toll on every aspect of my life personally and professionally. All I had left was my faith in God. In my spirit, I knew it was my turn to lay everything I had and everything I was on the altar. I released everything to His care: my marriage, my family, my business, my offices, my staff, and all of my material possessions. I had to take on the willing spirit of Abraham as he headed up the mountain with his beloved son. Abraham did not know how the story would end. He only knew that God was calling him to be willing to give everything, even his child.

I released everything to God without knowing where I would end up. During this tough season I learned so much about myself. I discovered that what I did professionally did not define who I was, nor did it determine my overall value. As a matter of fact, I had it backward. Who I was *personally* determined what I did professionally. My professional life was and is just a very small part of my identity. Yet in that moment of fear and frustration, this was not an easy truth to embrace. But God faithfully revealed to me that whether my business failed or succeeded, my value as a professional or human being was not at stake. No one could take away what I had accomplished, the mistakes I had made, and the lessons I had learned.

I wish for you this kind of growth and clarity. It truly was a point of epiphany in my life. I now have a clear understanding that we can do nothing perfect without God, because God is the one who has the perfect plan for our lives. He truly has a plan and purpose for our lives that we are living out every day. I have learned to live in peace whether I am in the valley or on top of the mountain taking in the view. What God has for me to do shall be done, and what God has for me to possess shall be mine. For Jesus is the author and finisher of our faith. He is our provider. Our job is to get up each day and walk in victory.

The Ultimate Gift

While we learn to enjoy sharing with others, we can never out-give God. He gave the most precious gift of all—His only Son. "For God so loved the world that He gave His only begotten Son, that whoever believes in Him should not perish but have ever-lasting life" (John 3:16). God is our role model. He gave us His best, and He is expecting us to give Him our best. Giving should be a privilege for us. And although we should not expect to receive anything in return, God is so good that He promises that if we keep His commandments, He will bless us.

God challenges us to try Him on the principles of giving. "'Will a man rob God? Yet you have robbed Me! But you say, "In what way have we robbed You?" In tithes and offerings. You are cursed with a curse, for you have robbed Me, even this whole nation. Bring all the tithes into the storehouse, that there may be food in My house, and try Me now in this,' says the LORD of hosts, 'if I will not open for you the windows of heaven and pour out for you such blessing that there will not be room enough to receive it'" (Malachi 3:8-10). God is looking for people He can trust with the blessings He has for His children. I challenge you to try God. Apply His principles on giving, and watch your life unfold and reach new levels of success.

Keep in mind, real success is not a big corner office. Real success is peace within every aspect of your life. Even as we give our best, our all, we should show God gratitude for who He is and the blessings He is about to send our way. When you follow God's will for your personal giving plan, you are investing in the life He made for you. In the financial world, we call this a guaranteed return on your investment.

Principle Prayer

Lord, help me realize all that I have to give. Grant me a listening heart so I can take my giving cues from You. I pray for obedience and integrity so that I may honor my responsibilities to give to Your house, Lord. I long for the joy that comes with selflessness. Remove my thoughts of accumulation to make room for thoughts of giving. You have called me to serve with my time, money, and self. These are my offerings. May they be acceptable to You, Giver of all. Amen.

$\mathcal{P}$rinciple in Practice

1. Give of yourself—find five new ways to do this.

2. Check your home for the type of love that lives there. If it is not the love God shares with us in 1 Corinthians 13, begin making the necessary changes.

3. Tithe on all your increases. Or "how you feel led to the church where you are being fed." If you are not currently tithing, tithe for 60 days. Challenge God and monitor His actions towards you.

4. Give your offerings based on your heart. Remember, offerings tell God how much you love and appreciate Him because the amount is not commanded.

5. Document what you are giving on a monthly basis. Include tithes, offerings, and gifts to other charities. Are you pleased with the amount you are giving?

6. Give up the areas of your life God is calling you away from. Surrender your entire life to His will.

*E*xpress Gratitude and Joy

Give thanks for who He is and who you are.
Praise Him before the blessings flow.

"Enter into His gates with thanksgiving, and
into His courts with praise. Be thankful to Him,
and bless His name."

PSALM 100:4

The essence of gratitude is all around us. Once little children know the words "Mom" and "Dad," we are quick to teach them "please" and "thank you." The golden rule for interviews is to send a handwritten thank-you note. We gather around our televisions on award-show nights so we can watch celebrities say "thank you" to people we have never heard of. Gratitude has always been a key practice in my personal and professional life—so I wondered why my first inclination was to jump from the principle of giving to the principle of blessing, completely bypassing gratitude.

Then it hit me...I tend to praise God *after* He has blessed me, rather than before. I never stopped to evaluate *when* I thanked the Lord during the seasons of my life. And now that I was looking at my faith journey, I realized I had the order backward all this time. God wants our praise and worship before He blesses us. By faith we are to praise and worship Him before, during, and after blessings come. It was an exciting realization for me.

Wanting to fully explore this idea, I spent several days in the Bible. Did God call us to offer our thanksgiving in a certain way? I wouldn't get my answer until a later day, when I came down with the flu. And just like God does...He waited for my silence, my willingness to listen before He began to share about gratitude in interesting ways. He placed the topic on the lips of those around me, in magazine articles, in conversations with friends, and in television shows. After watching a show with Juanita Bynun teaching about worship and praise, followed by CeCe Winans singing praises, I just had to call my prayer partner and share how God was revealing new things to me. But before I could get a word out, my friend was sharing how God had put gratitude on her heart. "God is looking for His people to worship Him." Her words were aligned with the heart and message God had been planting in my spirit. "Amen," I said.

From that point on, God had my full attention. My eyes were opened to a deeper and fuller understanding of gratitude. I felt the Holy Spirit leading me to take what I had believed about praise and worship and throw it out. There will be times in our lives when what God wants from us today is totally different from what He wanted five years ago or even last year.

A Heart of Gratitude

What exactly does it mean to have gratitude? And do you have it or feel it? Do you actually give it, or do you receive it into your spirit? Many people think gratitude is being thankful for who we are and what we have. While our thankfulness should cover the gifts God bestows on us, a successful woman is thankful not only for who she is and what she has but for the source of her blessings. That's right. She spends time getting to know and understand her Father in heaven, her Provider.

A spirit of gratitude comes from our hearts—that place inside where our feelings and emotions are housed. And whatever our minds choose to dwell on becomes the source of light or dark that affects our hearts. So at any given moment, your feelings, emotions, and actions convey the state of your spirit.

Have you ever reacted strongly to one thing when the emotion was meant for another? For example, have you ever become overly frustrated by a girlfriend's grumblings about a boyfriend when you are really upset about a conversation with your mother three days earlier? When we are operating in the flesh, our mind controls the heart's response. When we become born-again Christians, the Holy Spirit penetrates our hearts and controls our thoughts, intentions, emotions, and feelings along with our mind. The Holy Spirit draws us to God. "Create in me a clean heart, O God" (Psalm 51:10). If our hearts are clean, the Spirit can begin to operate in a totally new environment.

God gets our attention through our hearts, but if our minds are not transformed, then our hearts will change back to the old ways. That is why Romans 12:2 tell us, "Do not be conformed to this world, but be transformed by the renewing of your mind, that you may prove what is that good and acceptable and perfect will of God." Our minds have to be renewed so our hearts can also be renewed. To lead a successful life, a partnership between our minds and hearts must be nurtured.

Read the following Scripture over and over. This is a great starting place for you to train your mind in the ways of goodness and peace.

> Finally, brethren, whatever things are true, whatever things are noble, whatever things are just, whatever things are pure, whatever things are lovely, whatever things are of good report, if there is any virtue and if there is anything praiseworthy—meditate on these things. The things which you learned and received and heard and saw in me, these do, and the God of peace will be with you (Philippians 4:8-9).

Dance with David

When I think of the type of gratitude God wants us to have, I think of David. He was said to be a man after God's own heart (1 Samuel 13:14). The Bible does not tell us that David was perfect—in fact, he struggled greatly—but Scripture does present a picture of David's sincere love and gratitude for God. David loved to worship God so much that he danced before the Lord with all his might (2 Samuel 6:14). His love was so strong it moved his feet, his spirit, and his heart to a place of joyful expression. This is evident when you read many of the songs and poems David wrote in the book of Psalms.

David understood that our first duty is to be grateful to God in all circumstances. Even when we cannot see beyond our trial, even when we have only our faith to offer Him. Praise God for who He is instead of what He can do to fill your needs...or perceived needs. He already knows everything we need, so don't let your only time with Him be spent asking for blessings, lest you forget to save time to dance before Him in gratitude.

Almighty God

"For God is the King of all the earth; sing praises with understanding. God reigns over the nations; God sits on His holy throne" (Psalm 47:7-8). Your God...my God...is King over all things. He reigns over the nations and sits on His holy throne. He is our Father, our Savior, and our Redeemer. He is the Alpha and the Omega of life—our personal beginning and end. He created heaven and earth, man and woman, and all living creatures on the earth and in the sky. He is the love of our lives. We serve a God who is able to do exceedingly more than we could even think to request. Take my hand...join me as we celebrate this God who calls us His own.

Creator

Even before you get to the Principle in Practice section of this chapter, I have a little exercise for you. Pull out your favorite Bible translation and turn to Genesis 1:1-33. Let's just take a short walk together through the story of Creation. In case you have forgotten how phenomenal God is, this should bring it all back.

God spoke creation into being. He separated out day from night with a single command. He raised the firmament to divide the waters and to shape portions of land for His future creations. He sowed the earth with grass, herbs that yield seed, and fruit trees, and He carved out rolling hills, mountains, rivers, and streams.

To provide for future harvests, the Lord set in motion the birth of seasons. Spring, summer, fall, and winter overflow with beauty and purpose in the cycle of Creation. God blessed the sea and sky with exquisite living creatures to inhabit them. Then God brought forth living creatures according to their kind; cattle and creeping things and beasts of the earth.

God prepared the earth for those who would return His love with praise, worship, and the dance of gratitude: those who would be formed in His image. (See...we are His children. We even have our Father's likeness.) "And the Lord God formed man of the dust of the ground, and breathed into his nostrils the breath of life; and man became a living being" (Genesis 2:7).

From the very beginning, He was our provider. By placing man over all other creatures, He bestowed gifts of abundance, responsibility, and privilege. Then God gave Adam the gift of a helpmate so together they would be fruitful and multiply and fill the earth with others who could sing God's praises and live in abundance.

I find myself totally overwhelmed by the account of Genesis. God's love, power, and might are breathtaking. And yet so often we stand with our arms lifted high and open...not in a stance of praise but in a gesture of requesting more. We question when things don't go our way. Don't we see the wonders of Creation before us? Have we not embraced the God who formed us and provided all that we could ever need, including a relationship with our Creator? How could we not have great gratitude for such a God?

The Power of a Name

What names do you assign to your Lord? Do you make your offerings to a mighty God? Do you doubt His authority in your life? A successful person continues to learn, attend classes, stretch. A successful child of God gets to know her Savior so she can serve the King and understand the nature of her Lord.

As you look at the following Old Testament names for our Lord, let your mind and heart be transformed by the power of gratitude and wonder. Some translations provide the compound Jehovah name, while some other Bible versions provide the translated name.

- Jehovah-jireh—The Lord Shall Provide (Genesis 22:14)
- Jehovah-nissi—The Lord My Banner (Exodus 17:15)
- Jehovah-Elyon—The Lord Most High (Genesis 14:18-20)
- Jehovah-rophe—The Lord Our Healer (Exodus 15:26)
- Jehovah-shalom—The Lord Our Peace (Judges 6:24)

The Gift of the Journey

One December afternoon I was driving alone through a forest in Oregon on my way to a personal writing retreat. It was growing late, and I was becoming tired as I drove along the curvy coastal roads. My hands were firmly on the wheel, and I leaned forward with my shoulders hunched. I was totally focused on getting to my destination. As I went around a particularly tight curve I caught a glimpse of a majestic tree that reached heavenward. It was pointing me back to the Creator. And for the first time in over an hour, I noticed the awesome serenity of my surroundings. I thought to myself, *I spend so much time figuring out where I'm going, I miss out on where I am right now.*

I slowed the car down and began to look around at the lush hills, jagged rocks, and rushing waterfalls. *If I saw this as a painted image, I would want to wrap it up and take it on home...*I caught myself mid-thought and had to laugh; I was thinking ahead again. This moment was not created to be placed on a wall for later viewing. This moment was about worshiping God in my immediate circumstance. This gift was to be fully experienced right then and there. My destination did not seem nearly as important as my journey.

How many special moments had I already missed because my sights were set on the destination or deadline and not the journey or the process?

In my earlier years of faith, I would start my prayers with thanksgiving for my family, friends, and church, followed by my thanks for blessings like my home, businesses, car, opportunities, and so on. Today my prayers and even my thoughts and desires have changed. It is funny how God takes you through challenges to help you grow, to get your attention, and to prepare you for your destiny. Although I am still thankful for all those things, I am more thankful for the time and experiences I have with my family, friends, and others. I could drive right by waterfalls and breathtaking vistas or I could stop and be a witness of God's splendor.

Take time to enjoy the moments that add up to your lifetime. When you are in the car with your children or your husband, talk to them, ask questions, take advantage of such an opportunity. If you are standing in line at the grocery store, thank the Lord for nourishing your spirit and providing food for your family. Drive around your community and appreciate the people, scenery, and unique offerings of this place and time.

When God Says No

Isn't it wonderful to talk up God when things are going our way? You want to stop people in the street and speak about His miracles in your life. Your heart seeks new ways to glorify the Lord because He is worthy. But what about when God says no to something we have wanted? Are we grabbing people on the subway and shouting "hallelujah!" when our promotion falls through, when we struggle to make ends meet, when the man who promised "forever" has left the home? Are we still grateful to God when everything seems to be falling apart?

My experiences have truly tested my relationship with God. I admit I have been blessed beyond anything I could have imagined, but there is that part of me that starts to doubt when I cannot see His hand in a situation. When our daughter was having extreme migraines, my husband and I cried out for God's help. We spent many hours holding our little girl and offering words of comfort, but our prayers for a quick fix seemed to fall short of God's ears. We knew how to pray, but would prayer provide the immediate relief we so desperately wanted for Briana? I knew worse things were happening to other people every day, but that didn't change how protective and helpless I felt right then. I had to decide if I had enough faith to trust God with my daughter—the daughter He had saved in my womb. "For everyone to whom much is given, from him much will be required" (Luke 12:48). Would I praise and worship Him while everything in my life was not perfect? Yes. Because He had given me much, my faith was required whether God healed Briana in that moment, later, or never.

By faith we are to be at peace with praise and worship on our lips. Our belief will allow us to trust God's goodness at all times. "And we know that all things work together for good to those who love God, to those who are the called according to His purpose" (Romans 8:28). If we are called to His purpose, if our vision aligns with God's design for our life, then our struggle will be used for good. Do you know that what God has for you is better than anything you could want for yourself? If you are facing a trial, a loss, a time of doubt, let your past encounters with His love rush to your memory. Ralph Waldo Emerson wrote, "All I have seen teaches me to trust the Creator for all I have not seen." Express your gratitude for past lessons of faith that sustain you in difficult times.

Daily Gratitude

Taking on the spirit of gratitude is a daily choice. When you arise in the morning, you can either conjure up visions of what could go wrong with the day, or you can thank God for the opportunities ahead to seek Him and praise Him.

Often people ask me why I am so happy. Many ask me this question because they are aware of the challenges I have been through. Yet the question always surprises me, because I wonder why people are *not* happy. I don't have a secret…I have faith. I have my Father in heaven who cares for me. I have a strong, loving family. I am in my right mind (most days). I have my health and abilities. And while my life certainly isn't perfect, I choose to focus on all the blessings, including the trials that draw me closer to my God. This daily spirit of gratitude motivates me to appreciate the good things and trust God to handle the difficult situations.

God is operating on our behalf morning, noon, and night. "Therefore I say to you, do not worry about your life, what you will eat or what you will drink; nor about your body, what you will put on. Is not life more than food and the body more than clothing?" (Matthew 6:25). "Therefore do not worry, saying, 'What shall we eat?' or 'What shall we drink?' or 'What shall we wear?' For after all these things the Gentiles seek. For your heavenly Father knows that you need all these things. But seek first the kingdom of God and His righteousness, and all these things shall be added to you" (Matthew 6:31-33). Do you worry about minor details when God is calling you to bigger purposes? Make a choice today whether you will dance through life to the soundtrack of worry or gratitude.

During the services at my church, Bishop Kenneth Ulmer often says, "You don't know, like I know, what He has done for me." We all have our own stories of what God has done. Are you taking time to notice the unfolding of your own story? Are you on intimate terms with what the Lord has done for you? When I think of His goodness and mercy toward me, my soul shouts *hallelujah!* If you and I had a thousand tongues, we could not praise Him enough. If we had a thousand days, we could not praise Him enough. But as long as we have the gift of another day, we will keep on trying...because as growing children of God, once we know "Abba," the next thing to learn is "thank you."

Principle Prayer

Creator. Majesty. King of Kings. I am grateful that You call me Your own. I have done nothing to deserve Your love. You have done everything to deserve my spirit of gratitude. Give me clarity to appreciate every moment of my life. Help me fill my mind with all that is pure and good. Let joy flow from my heart to those who do not yet have Your hope in their lives. When doubt creeps into my spirit, may I reflect on my own story. Nobody knows, like I know, what You, Abba Father, have done for me. Amen.

$\mathcal{P}$rinciple in Practice

1. For one week, start each day by listing ten personal reasons to praise God.

2. Pray for a heart of gratitude and joy, and be aware of how you change.

3. Read Romans 8:28. Read it again...and let it sink in to your spirit.

4. Choose a Scripture to memorize and reflect on for the entire month. Let the verse be your true, noble, and pure meditation to nourish your mind and heart.

5. Take notice of how often you choose worry over gratitude. Plan a day to completely embrace the spirit of gratitude. You might just discover the principle of success you have been missing.

6. Before the blessings are upon you, praise the Lord. If you do not feel blessed, praise the Lord. And if you face a trial that draws you to Him, praise the Lord.

*R*eceive Your Blessing

*Notice, receive, and share each blessing
that comes from the Lord.*

"The blessing of the LORD makes one rich, and
He adds no sorrow with it."

PROVERBS 10:22

Late one night I climbed into bed exhausted from a long and
hectic day. Before my eyelids succumbed to gravity's pull, I spent
a few minutes journaling about recent difficulties for myself and
others. My pen hit the paper and out poured everything. Fresh tears
fell onto my black-and-white versions of stories that would have
read like fiction had I not known these people and their struggles
so intimately. I thought back to each phone call filled with trem-
bling voices and expressions of pain and anguish. Through prayer,
long conversations, and more prayer I offered support to these
family members and friends as they called from cancer centers,
police stations, and a funeral home.

I thought about Job again. How it is possible to be awestruck
by pain. If compassion and empathy are a part of our Christian

character, can we take on so much that we have no room in our hearts for another pain? If so, I was there. I kept giving these wounds to God, but they remained in my spirit. I was weary and trying to find my way to the foot of the cross. As I placed my journal by my bed, the weight of all those requests and needs still felt heavy on my heart. This was a season of change and pain for myself and many people in my circle of friends, family, and community. We were all waiting for a blessing. Any blessing.

Looking for a Blessing

Once again, I had a major principle all wrong and God was ready to make a bold point. Did you see those "message from God" billboards that popped up all over the nation? Well, I felt as though every turn I was taking along my new road had one of those huge, impossible-to-miss signs. Sometimes I was rushing by too fast to comprehend the message. But in a season of hardship, I was slowed to a crawl...crawling toward the foot of the cross...and finally ready to hear what God wanted to teach me.

My head echoed with the promises I had made to God just over a year prior to this season of struggle. I vowed that I would be available to Him for the rest of my life...in trial and in blessing. So now I had to face a test. Was I willing to learn the true meaning of blessing while I was crawling? Yes. I knew I needed to press on, not only for myself, but so I could continue to encourage my friends and loved ones to be strong.

I prayed for discernment. I prayed to read God's messages and His Word without any preconceived theories and theologies. I meditated on the Beatitudes and other verses to discover what blessing really meant to the Christian journey. *Bring it on. And don't sugar coat it, Lord.* I didn't have to say that part...He had no such intention.

Faith Shopping Network

What I knew about blessing came from various church ser-
mons and how my friends viewed the concept. The "name it, claim
it, and frame it" philosophy had been prevalent in much of my
life. The "If we do *this*, God will do *this*. If we ask God for what
we want, He will be faithful" mindset initially felt very comfortable to me...I think because it felt a bit like shopping. And I love
to shop. *Let me see...I would love this life in a humble shade of
lavender, and let's accessorize it with these accomplishments. Here...I
have a picture torn from a magazine of the life I want. I choose that,
Lord.* I know I am oversimplifying the concept, and the comparison to shopping is tongue-in-cheek. But ladies, I know people
who embrace this theory passionately and then wait for a new life
to be delivered C.O.D.—that is, Christ on Demand.

Now, however, this philosophy seems incomplete to me. As I
watch people await their delivery (and believe me, I have spent
time on the front porch of my life watching for my own neatly
packaged "new life"), I wonder...*if this is of God, why are we still
praying and searching for what we named, claimed, and framed years
ago?* I have so many old claims that I have forgotten the point of
some of them. This led me to start asking questions and searching
for the truth about being blessed and finding the path to living
with blessing.

Getting What We Need

I began my journey by looking back over my shoulder at my
life. Hindsight provides wisdom, right? How had God blessed me?
There have been times when I asked God to provide for me, and
He moved within my circumstances right away. Other times a
change would take place, but much later and when I too had gone

through change enough to deal with it. But more times than not I have petitioned God and watched while, you got it, nothing happened. *Did You not hear me, Lord?* So I would make my plea once again. My request was met with God's "no." You see, God—as in God: Creator of the Universe—knows a few things about human nature. And He knows that, when it comes to our claim about what we need, there is a conflict between our personal motives and the greater good, between our needs and the needs of God's plan.

Basically, about 80 percent of the time, we don't know what we need. At least that seems to be my average. My perspective can be so far off track that God sees fit to respond with the complete opposite of my request. Now, that is humbling. Have you ever stood pointing at door number one, certain the promotion and the vacation cruise will enhance your resume and life, and God opens squeaky door number two to reveal something resembling a "you're fired" pink slip and one-way ticket to the unemployment line? You think, "Did my request get muddled? Do I need to take courses in How to Pray and Influence God?" No. You probably did fine. You just missed the point. In Philippians 4:11-13, Paul reveals his faith secret: "I have learned to be content whatever the circumstances. I know what it is to be in need, and I know what it is to have plenty. I have learned the secret of being content in any and every situation, whether well fed or hungry, whether living in plenty or in want. I can do everything through him who gives me strength" (NIV).

The life of success does not have to be delivered to you. It can be right where you are, no matter the situation (Paul was in prison when he shared this revelation). In plenty. In little. In abundance. In want. In freedom. In chains. When you have the Lord's peace, you have what you need in all circumstances. When you recognize this, that is success.

The curious and miraculous part about that squeaky door number two…it actually could lead us to the destination we envisioned from the start. The problem is that we ask for things the way a child asks, with complete disregard for logic, wisdom, and understanding. "I like the pony. Give me the pony now." That child might end up being a veterinarian in Kentucky in 25 years, but he sure isn't going to get a pony for his fifth birthday. You see? The answer is no…and yes. That is how awesome our God is.

So, God bless you. I mean it. God blesses you when He seems to be taking you way off course. Sometimes it is a shortcut over a rocky mountain pass, other times it is a slow boat to the Arctic. Either way, friend, you will be blessed. Each route has a different set of circumstances that has to be addressed. Knowing this won't necessarily ease all of your concerns or answer your questions, but it is a start. And whichever route you are on right now…it is okay to confess, "I don't understand."

Lord, I Do Not Understand

I am surrounded by women in the workplace, on the road while traveling, at church, and in my circle of friends. And without exception, each one of them has faced moments when they cry out in shame and confusion, "Lord, I do not understand." And from there, the questions flow: Why is God allowing all of this to happen? Why must I take the long way and experience so many difficult situations? I do not understand. Where is my blessing?

Women strive to be the all-in-all for everyone in their lives. We work so hard to prove ourselves in various arenas that to utter the words "I don't understand" feels like the sure kiss of failure. But this confession is the act of a successful woman. If you are in business, you know that the employee who asks the hard questions and strives to understand a situation is the one who will achieve. So be proud of yourself when you must completely humble yourself before the Lord. Say it. Say it a couple times. "Lord, I do not understand what You are doing." Now complete that sentence with "...but I trust You. And I know You are blessing me." Congratulations, you are learning what you need to have a successful life!

Your Footsteps Are Ordered

Proverbs 20:24 says, "A man's steps are of the LORD. How then can a man understand his own way?" It isn't our job to understand what God is doing and where He is taking us. It is our job to trust Him and be grateful for the journey. We talked about God creating each one of us with a purpose and plan of our very own. God's intention is for us to live out this purpose every day. Think of God as a schoolmaster who has daily assignments for us to accomplish. He already knows we will go to the bookstore, the grocery store, the business conference; He knows we will bump into an old friend, a colleague, and the daughter of a neighbor; He has viewed the conversation that inspires our vision, the cancellation of a project, and the chance to mentor a young girl with a vision. These encounters and events do not happen by accident. So don't respond to them as if they are casual occurrences. Look for God's way in each moment and in each decision.

Keep in mind: His ways are not our ways. And you don't have to figure it all out. This insight should free us to embrace our spiritual principles and rest in the blessing of each opportunity. God sits and rules over the entire world. While we can only see a very small piece of the puzzle, God sees and shapes the million other pieces...some of which are being made to fit and complete your own picture. His primary goal is to spread the gospel all over the world so that people will have the opportunity to accept Jesus Christ as Lord and Savior. This is the good He is working out through obedient, purposeful lives. He wants your life to be one of those.

When God requires us to stretch, grow, and face the fire, it is for a reason. "Behold, I have refined you, but not as silver; I have tested you in the furnace of affliction" (Isaiah 48:10). When the heat reshapes and refines us, this is a blessing. You might be called to give up something you love. You might need to view a circumstance with different eyes and a deeper faith. You might be entrusted with material wealth which adds the burden of greater responsibility to your plate. These are all different kinds of blessings. He is preparing us for the role we are to play. The preparation process must be endured and embraced for us to serve the purpose God planted within our spirits.

I Surrender All

Whether I am standing in the kitchen or the boardroom, I am an analytical person. When everyone is pointing to the brightly colored kite in the sky, I am the one wondering how the person on the ground maneuvered it to reach such heights. I am the one looking around for power lines and troubleshooting. I am the one trying to recall how the frame of a kite affects its flight. I am the one who might really bother you if you just wanted to enjoy the sight of the kite.

Now, add perfectionism to analytical and they equal hair loss. Why? Because this combination of traits makes me want to pull my hair out. It used to anyway. I share this because many women are the same way. Though we are afraid to say "I don't understand," we are terrified to turn over anything to anyone. After all, we are well-practiced jugglers tossing about the needs of others, responsibilities of home and office, and daily personal demands.

Meanwhile, we are putting out fires and anticipating those that might rage in the near future. You probably are becoming tense as you read this either because a) this reminds you of something on your to-do list, or b) because you know what I am about to ask of you. Actually, God asks this of all successful women. Drumroll, please. Surrender. Yes. I said surrender.

Whether I am in the heat of a difficult battle or in a position of rest waiting for the next one, I have learned to accept the situation and surrender it to God's hands. Now I can live with the peace that surpasses all understanding that Philippians 4:6-7 talks about. "Be anxious for nothing, but in everything by prayer and supplication with thanksgiving, let your requests be made known to God; and the peace of God, which surpasses all understanding, will guard your hearts and minds through Christ Jesus."

For those of us who have experienced a controlling earthly father, it can be difficult to give yourself and your journey over to the heavenly Father. God is in control. He is not controlling. He provided the gift of free will and the peace of His mercy and forgiveness. Please go to Him as His daughter and seek to learn a new meaning for Father...Abba. He is loving, caring, and wants the very best for you. If I am speaking to your personal journey, I know what you are going through. As you apply these principles to your life, perhaps the most important thing you will take away is the truth that God loves you and wants you to have the real success I describe at the beginning of this book. You are loved, sister. Take that blessing and hold it close.

A Plan for Blessing

God makes His plan to bless us very clear. "I will make you a great nation; I will bless you and make your name great; and you shall be a blessing. I will bless those who bless you, and I will curse him who curses you; and in you all the families of the earth shall be blessed" (Genesis 12:2). God is blessing Abraham and his family, and He promises to bless all of us through Abraham. Because we are descendants of Abraham, we are blessed through our family lineage. Our family ties with Abraham, the father of the nations, come with prepackaged benefits. God blessed Abraham spiritually, emotionally, physically, and materially. We are actually too limited when we pray for God to bless us in only one area.

An Identity Crisis

While we are praying for a blessing, most of us are walking right by countless other blessings because we feel we don't truly deserve them. Voices from the past say "good things from God are not for you." You started telling yourself that lie after a few failures. So many women have confided in me that they are afraid to step out in faith. They question whether they have what it takes to pursue their goals. Years of doubt have kept them from knowing their potential, their dreams, and their God.

I believe many women struggle with this identity crisis. The world has taught us to focus on external self instead of eternal soul. Our dress size or paycheck takes on a bizarre level of importance while we ignore the size of our gifts and talents. No wonder we don't know ourselves or the potential God has planted in us. He created each and every one of us the way He wanted us to be. If you pay attention, your mind, body, and spirit will be in line with what God created you to do. So, while you are working on the hair, the weight, the diet, and the muscle tone, be sure you are moving forward with you dreams and destiny.

Look back in the previous chapter at that list of Old Testament names for God, or better yet, look at the Old Testament and gather and study the many names for God. Knowing who God is allows you to know who you are. Your Daddy is the King. Therefore, you are a princess destined for greatness and victory. Our Father has already set the stage for our success. Empty yourself of doubt or regret. Make room to be replenished and refilled with blessings.

Start Small

The moment I walked into the market, the fragrance drifting from the flower cart intoxicated me. I was on a quest to select a perfect bouquet to adorn my hallway table for the baby shower I was hosting that afternoon. My eyes scanned many exotic choices, but I was drawn to some purple tulips. Next to ornate orchids, tulips can come across as simple, practical. But a closer look revealed petal color so rich and deep, it looked and felt like velvet. Elated, I gathered as many as I could carry. I smiled the entire drive home, not only because my friend would love this extra touch, but because the God who tended to such detail in a flower was the God who tended to my life. He painted the sturdy tulip with delicate brilliance to bring pleasure to our lives. I realized how long it had been since I had paid attention to small blessings.

Blessing means to invoke divine care. I truly believe God is beginning to release the riches of the wicked to the righteous, and Christians will be blessed with major blessings. But before we can get to the releasing of the riches, we must first deal with the day-to-day life issues that prevent us from being anywhere near ready to accept the rich blessings God has for us.

Real blessing—like real success—is built on faith, not material accumulation. This faith allows you to look past your circumstances to believe everything will work out for good. Faith lets us say, "This situation has a blessing in it for me. I just have to look a little closer at what God is doing." Be patient and wait for the blessing to reveal itself. God is trying to get us to pay attention to the blessings we have taken for granted.

When we wake up in the morning, we start pondering our worries and completely miss the miracle of a new day. We breathe in and out, rarely in awe of the air available to us. Our legs, arms, hands, lungs, heart, liver, intestines, bladder, kidneys, and all of our other body parts function, and we make full use of this blessing without acknowledging it. Only when you or someone you love faces physical struggle do you learn to be grateful for health. That is the problem with a basically good life...until things are taken away from us, we don't give our daily miracles much thought.

I sincerely believe we must learn to appreciate the little blessings God provides before He will expand our territory by giving us the opportunity to enjoy greater blessings.

Blessings in Hindsight

I began an introspective process several months before I turned 40. In my mind, the very visible number of candles marked an invisible halfway point in my life. This life assessment was long overdue. I highly recommend it. Reflection inspires awareness. Awareness inspires change, renewal, and appreciation. Looking at my life under a microscope forced me to be totally honest. I was extremely proud of some accomplishments and times of strength and faith. I also had to face the two-headed monster named failure and disappointment.

My introspection covered all areas of my life. Old hurts resurfaced and times of joy also made their presence known as I analyzed my feelings about what had or had not happened. By the grace of God, I have come through some difficult experiences. By investing some time and spiritual effort acknowledging these seasons of hardship, I uncovered the lost value and blessing of these situations. No, hindsight did not add rays of sunshine to dark moments, but it did shed light on the blessing of surviving and persevering...a blessing so powerful, the sheer realization of it took my breath away.

I recalled a time when I was so frustrated that I questioned if God really knew me. I wondered if He understood how I felt and what I was going through. *If He loves me and I am His child, why would He allow me to hurt this way?* I had been operating under the assumption that once I became a Christian I would not panic, cry, or slip into depression. I did not understand what God was doing in my life. The life of salvation seemed more difficult than life before I was saved.

I encourage you to pray for direction as you reflect on your life. Ask God to point out the blessings you have missed. If you focus solely on failures or sorrows, you will remain in the past and the momentum of your purpose can come to a halt. If you focus on the blessings that accompanied or were born out of these trials, you are gathering strength for your journey forward. Each blessing becomes a stepping stone toward that vision you have been given.

Spiritual Cardiograms

When I retraced the jagged lines representing the peaks and valleys in my life, it was as if I were examining a cardiogram. How appropriate this comparison was...the highs and lows of these lines reflected the rhythm and condition of my heart for God. My seasons of blessings clearly lined up with times when I was in step with God's purpose for my life. When I was spending time focused on Him and not myself, I was on track with my targeted goals and accomplishments. The more time I was spending with Him, the more successful I was becoming. And by successful, I mean I was spiritually in tune enough to see the blessings, big or small, in my circumstances. When I was off track spiritually, I sidestepped my vision and reached for rewards rather than blessings.

Our God is a good Father; He does not entertain our requests to receive everything "here and now." Every blessing is released at its appropriate time. God will bless us next year with blessings He would not give to us this year because it was not the appropriate season. If our blessings are released to us before we are ready, they can go unnoticed or unappreciated. Why would God waste a blessing?

Eat Your Manna

It can be easy to ignore a blessing from God. We have probably even complained about a blessing—like the Israelites who became tired of manna from heaven. Because it was plentiful, they mistook this miracle for something ordinary. "The rabble with them began to crave other food, and again the Israelites started wailing and said, 'If only we had meat to eat! We remember the fish we ate in Egypt at no cost—also the cucumbers, melons, leeks, onions and garlic. But now we have lost our appetite; we never see anything but this manna!'" (Numbers 11:4-6 NIV).

Our manna, our daily diet of blessing, is sent from God's hands to sustain us as we pursue our purpose. If we pass on the manna, saying, "No, thanks. I'll wait for a pizza with meat topping," we will be waiting a long time. And getting mighty hungry for a blessing in the meantime. The bigger blessings are not intended to line up with what we want; they line up with what God wants for us. We can pray day and night for our list of goodies and rewards, but our blessings have to line up with the work we are destined to do.

So say grace...and eat your manna.

The Planting of a Life

While my spiritual cardiogram had revealed the condition of my heart toward God, it also revealed a pattern of God. "To everything there is a season, a time for every purpose under heaven" (Ecclesiastes 3:1). Though I have read this verse many times, I had not directly, intimately related it to my life. I felt a security I had not known in a long time. While I had given the "God is in control" theory a lot of lip service over the years, the distinct seasons and the wonder of God's plan were just becoming reality to me.

Now that I have lived in California for quite a few years, the changing seasons are only noticed in slight fashion modifications and in the schedule of my daughter's school year. But the impact is nothing to what I experience when I return to the Midwest or the East Coast, where vibrant colors herald the arrival of fall, or shadows and chilly winds usher in winter's dormancy. Each trip to these regions reminds me of God's orchestration of the seasons and how they serve a purpose in creating and sustaining life.

Avid gardeners have a deep understanding of seasons because the physical conditions of weather cycles and the earth's surface directly affect how and when life and growth can take place. Let's look at our lives in the form of a garden to better understand and appreciate how we go through seasons of planting and harvest and how blessing only comes after seasons of preparation and dormancy.

Planning

The first season is a season of planning. This is a time for gathering information, knowledge, and making decisions that will affect the success of the garden's growth. We'll choose a vegetable garden for this illustration. Now we have a lot more decisions to make…which vegetables grow best in our regions, do they need sun or shade, how much space is required between the rows, how big should our garden plot be to accommodate the future harvest? Spiritually, this is our time to learn more about God, His purpose, and what walk-on-water faith is all about.

Preparation

Now that we understand the needs of this garden, we enter a season of preparation. We used our heads, now we must use our hands in labor to prepare the soil, clear the weeds, and add fertilizers and nourishment to the land. In other words, we must put in some work before we can invite people over for homemade salsa. This season of vision requires tools and resources to make our goals possible. No shortcuts can be taken during this time, or the life we hope to grow will not take root, will not thrive, will not produce.

Planting

Ahh. Thank goodness the preparation is done…now maybe we can get to the good stuff. Funny thing is, some of us love the earlier stages, the planning, strategizing, and goal setting. Others of us live for this latter part of the process. Seeing the physical manifestation of our efforts is fulfilling. This third season is reserved for planting and watering. The seeds must be put in the ground and cared for on a daily basis. Your spiritual life needs to be tended to just like this. God's Word will not take root unless you care for it with living water and attention. This season requires faithfulness and a steadfast heart as we wait and watch for the appearance of new life to spring forth from the soil.

Harvest

The fourth and final season is the season of harvest. The time we have all waited for. We can now reap the blessing of abundance and, in turn, experience the blessings of sharing, giving, and extending our wealth. The successful woman recognizes that her hard work and vision flourished under the care of God's timing and His plan of provision. She sees the harvest of blessing and is grateful.

Full Circle

"Therefore, my beloved brethren, be steadfast, immovable, always abounding in the work of the Lord, knowing that your labor is not in vain in the Lord" (1 Corinthians 15:58). There is no replacement for hard work, and one cannot rush the seasons. We can try to avoid them altogether, and just plan, plant, or prepare any ol' time we like, but I guarantee you will reap only a portion of what God intended for your harvest. When we embrace the process and experience the reason for each season, we can anticipate success.

The Cost of Being Blessed

I can just hear the response this section heading is inciting. "Now that we know how to recognize and appreciate blessings, you want to tell us there is a downside?" Although I used this Scripture earlier, I will repeat it so God's Word can break it to you: "For everyone to whom much is given, from him much will be required" (Luke 12:48). Don't look at me. I am just the messenger.

Well...the messenger and someone who can say "Been there, done that, still living it."

No matter the size or shape of a blessing, it arrives with a requirement: The blessing that arises as a result of spiritual success is meant to be shared.

Money Talks...But What Does It Say?

I believe many Christians have a skewed view of the blessing of material wealth. For many years I only desired to have a comfortable life because I had been taught that the rich cannot get into heaven. I aspired to make just enough money to pay my bills and set aside a little for my future. Most Christians live this way, yet God has so much more for us. Please do not get me wrong. I am not challenging moderate lifestyles. Because even if/when you increase your wealth and territory, you are still called to be a wise steward.

I believe that the way people choose to live is related to their personal calling. You can earn $400,000 a year and live simply by allocating resources to others and by creating a way of life that does not require that many zeros. If you think a bank account full of money is telling you to forget your original vision and start going for the good stuff, then you are giving your money too much power in your life. Money should not change your calling; it should only serve to provide a means for achieving that calling.

Your purpose and vision might involve financial abundance. This will not mean you are more successful than women who make less; that would be the world's standard. All women who are willing to let God lead them to a new dimension in their lives will experience the most important wealth of all...spiritual riches. This standard will guide them as they pursue a ministry, a business, a goal.

The cost of wealth is great responsibility. We can ask God to show us how to invest our money and bring in 20, 30, and 40 percent returns. Allow God to show you how to buy that first home and increase your assets. I know from experience that by God's hand alone we can be shown how to start our own business and grow the business's annual revenue to $10-, $20-, $50-, and even $100-million-dollar companies.

When I was afraid money would undermine my spiritual purpose, I had not really studied God's Word. Jesus does not say it is impossible for a rich person to make it into heaven. He said it is difficult. "'Assuredly, I say to you that it is hard for a rich man to enter the kingdom of heaven. And again I say to you, it is easier for a camel to go through the eye of a needle than for a rich man to enter the kingdom of God'" (Matthew 19:23-24).

The portion of Scripture often left out of this lesson is the last part. "With God all things are possible" (verse 26). If we keep our focus on God and understand our provision comes only from Him and not from our own doing, money does not keep us from His presence.

With the right attitude we can remain humble and grateful for all the blessings that are given to us. The disciple Peter spoke up and said, "See, we have left all and followed you. Therefore what shall we have?" (Matthew 19:27). Jesus answers in verse 29 that "everyone who has left houses or brothers or sisters or father or mother or wife or children or lands, for My name's sake, shall receive a hundredfold, and inherit eternal life."

God has never had an issue with us having money. The problem occurs when the money has us. We get into trouble when we depend on money instead of God. "Command those who are rich in this present age not to be haughty, nor to trust in uncertain riches but in the living God, who gives us richly all things to enjoy" (1 Timothy 6:17). If we are not careful, money can become our primary focus.

Power and access to powerful people can be bought with notoriety and wealth. Monetary value ushers folks into the hierarchy of movers and shakers, and it turns their names and resumes into dinner party gossip and golf course discourse. New friends pop up everywhere because even perceived associations offer a taste of status or a ray of the limelight. Money doesn't just affect the behavior of friends and strangers, it can trigger self-deception. We might start wearing an invisible cape and considering ourselves more than human—invincible. Nothing and no one can stop us now. *Point out the tallest building, please. I'd like to leap over it in a single bound on my way to the country club.* Before we know it, our humility and sense of reality take their own flying leap...out the window.

Show Me (What to Do With) the Money

Money only magnifies the person you are already. If you are an excessive person, money will just give you a bigger outlet for displays of excessive behavior. If you are a kind, loving, and giving person, money will allow you to show more kindness and love through the wonderful gifts you now have the ability to give. Proverbs 22:2 tells us, "The rich and the poor have this in common, the LORD is the maker of them all." God created the rich woman and the poor woman. One is not better than the other or worse than the other...not until actions reveal the motives of the heart. If there is a problem ignited by wealth, don't blame God. Having money can and should be very positive as long as we depend on Almighty God instead of the almighty dollar.

Philanthropy, charity, ministry, and innovation turn material wealth into spiritual wealth for those who suffer among us. Extra resources allow us to bless our families, friends, community, and ourselves. I truly believe God wants to bless more and more believers with financial wealth so we can be a greater blessing to the body of Christ. On a larger scale, God is using money from believers to spread the Good News of Jesus Christ all over the world. People who may not have had the opportunity before will receive the gospel, become saved, and enter into heaven through resources funded by you and me. God is opening the door to a new season, where financial wealth will flow through believers to build the kingdom of believers all over the entire world. For such a time as now!

Principle Prayer

Lord, I am blessed because You are my Savior. I have value because I am Your child. Lead me away from the temptation to trade this value and wealth for material riches. If my vision leads to a time of wealth and material accumulation, guard my heart and mind from the deception that can follow worldly success. May I continue to see Your peace as the greatest fortune. And may the blessing of sharing be a blessing I embrace fully. You call me to sacrifice, Lord. In return, I know I will receive a hundredfold in Your kingdom. You are mighty. Amen.

*P*rinciple in Practice

1. During your season of hardship, keep looking for the blessing.

2. If you are looking for a new life with a "name it, claim it, frame it" mindset, you need to evaluate what God desires for your life. Await His vision, not one of your own desires.

3. Look at your own spiritual cardiogram. What did you miss the first time around that you can hold on to now?

4. If you do achieve financial wealth, you will need God's wisdom and protection. Think of five ways you would turn money into spiritual wealth.

5. What "manna" have you been tossing aside all along? To live a life of success—a life of God's peace and fulfillment—you need to receive manna with a grateful spirit.

6. Examine your life and ask God to remove anything that is keeping you from His abundance. You are a part of the kingdom God is building up in this season. Thank Him for that and prepare your heart to be made worthy.

For Such a Time as Now

Your season is upon you.

"To everything there is a season, a time for every purpose under heaven."

ECCLESIATES 3:1

"And let us not grow weary while doing good, for in due season we shall reap if we do not lose heart."

GALATIANS 6:9

It has been an incredible journey sharing these ten spiritual principles with you. I pray that each one enhances your life and gives you a better understanding of how much God loves you and wants to bless you. It is His desire that you live an abundant life right here on earth. Are you prepared, right now, to start living the life of success God has planned for you? If these ten principles are a part of your spiritual life, then the success of God's peace and purpose will be upon you.

Let's Celebrate Your Success

Send out the invitations for the victory party. Order the cake and balloons because it is time for a grand celebration. It is time to celebrate your hard work. Get ready because success is just around the corner. Your miracles are on their way!

The Holy Spirit is waiting to usher you through open doors and into the presence of the living God. Be ready to step out of the religious box and serve Him with your whole heart. It is time to begin a radical pursuit of your purpose and vision.

Do you feel the tingling sensation of a plan formulating in the depths of your spirit? You might sense that God is preparing a great thing. Perhaps a recent decision or transition has planted the seed for a new life vision. Some of us are ready to harvest after waiting for God's perfect timing. Whichever season you are in, God has strengthened you through storms of difficulty. You are still standing, my friend—and this is your testimony. A testimony that will bless people near and far. You have survived the valleys of struggle and surveyed the heights of triumph. Let's celebrate the season of blessing that is upon you. Let's rejoice in what God is about to do in your life.

As I said earlier, I believe the day and time has come when God is releasing the wealth of the wicked to the righteous. Believers are stepping into positions of power and authority as never before. A new dimension of victory is on your horizon as God uses contemporary methods to inspire the weary back to the fold and strengthen the faithful. God is not interested in just having church. He is building up new ministries, Christian businesses, and entrepreneurs to go out into the world and share the gospel in word and deed. The success God calls you to is a part of this bigger success story.

Know and Remember Who You Are

When you move through times of uncertainty, remember you are royalty—the daughter of the Lord of Lords and King of Kings.

You are also a servant who has been given the opportunity to obey God's will. Set your natural gifts and talents in motion, and they will lead to a life rich in meaning. Plan, prepare, plant, and harvest all the blessings God has for you to hold and to share.

Not so long ago, God whispered to me, "For such a time as now." And I knew my vision was to be realized within His will. Sharing this message with you is a part of that vision. Our paths have crossed, and we each have a purpose to be fulfilled that will serve God's perfect plan. Just imagine what God has in store for you. But remember that God's plans for goodness and peace are beyond our human imagination. Don't limit what God is about to do. God created your vision and dreams for such a time as now. God created *you* for such a time as now.

Let us rejoice and be glad.

$\mathcal{N}$otes

What Is Real Success?
1. Madeleine L'Engle, *Walking on Water* (Wheaton, IL: Harold Shaw Publishers, 1980), p. 31.

Spiritual Principle Three—Pray Without Ceasing
1. Renita J. Weems, *Listening for God* (New York, NY: Touchstone, 1999), p. 67.

Spiritual Principle Four—Believe in Your Purpose
1. T.D. Jakes, *Maximize the Moment* (New York, NY: Berkley Books, 1999), pp. 202-03.

Spiritual Principle Five—Follow Your Vision
1. Og Mandino, *The Greatest Salesman in the World* (New York, NY: Bantam Books, 1985), p. 90.

Spiritual Principle Six—Model Integrity
1. Laurie Beth Jones, *Jesus, Entrepreneur* (New York, NY: Three Rivers Press, 2001), p. xx.

Spiritual Principle Eight—Give Along the Way
1. Henri Nouwen, *Compassion: A Reflection on the Christian Life* (New York, NY: Doubleday, 1983), p. 126.

Victoria Lowe is a nationally recognized and celebrated business owner with a passion for building up the kingdom and sharing a triumphant message for every person who has a dream to know and do God's best. For information about Victoria Lowe and her speaking ministry, please write to Victoria at:

Victoria Lowe Ministries
300 Corporate Pointe
Suite 300
Culver City, CA 90230

Phone: (310) 846-5110

Or visit the official ministry website:
victorialoweministries.com

Other Lowe Enterprises: (310) 846-5110

- *All About Marketing, LLC*
  A full-service marketing company focused on growing companies by building strong brand images.

- *Well Said, LLC*
  A conference-management and speaker-selection company.

- *Risk Works, LLC*
  A risk-management company designed to assess, establish, and manage all aspects of corporate risk (safety programs, risk assessment, workers' compensation management, etc.).

Other Good Harvest House Reading

THE DIVA PRINCIPLE
by *Michelle McKinney Hammond*

Divine Inspiration for a Victorious Attitude…Michelle McKinney Hammond serves up the 4-1-1 on how to get and keep a victorious attitude—one entrenched in divine wisdom. She shows readers how to excel in every area of life by mastering the art of diva-tude!

THE POWER OF A PRAYING® WOMAN
by *Stormie Omartian*

Stormie's deep knowledge of Scripture and candid examples from her own prayer life provide guidance for women who seek to trust God with deep longings and cover every area of life with prayer.

RADICALLY OBEDIENT, RADICALLY BLESSED
by *Lysa TerKeurst*

Lysa TerKeurst shares personal stories and biblical insights to reflect the blessing that comes with complete obedience to Christ. This is an invitation to boldly ask for and expect more from the Christian life.

LIFE MANAGEMENT FOR BUSY WOMEN
by *Elizabeth George*

Admitting to being disorganized when she was in her 20s, Elizabeth shares the love and patience of God and the transforming power of His Word and Spirit that taught her the principles of life management.

BECOMING A WOMAN WHO LISTENS TO GOD
by *Sharon Jaynes*

Everyday life is loud with ringing phones, blaring TVs, and yelling children. Women find themselves longing for time away from it all so they can really hear God. Using wit, Southern charm, and wisdom, Sharon invites women everywhere to explore answers to the heartcry, "How can I hear the voice of God?"

HARVEST HOUSE
PUBLISHERS